The life and career of Steve Ballmer

From Microsoft Maverick to Billionaire Visionary. The Unstoppable Rise of a Tech Titan

Daniel J. Smith

Copyright © Daniel J. Smith 2025

No part of this publication may be reproduced, distributed, or transmitted in any form or by any means, including photocopying, recording, or other electronic or mechanical methods, without the prior written permission of the publisher, except in the case of brief quotations embodied in critical reviews and certain other noncommercial uses permitted by copyright law.

Table Of Contents

Introduction

Chapter One: Early Life and Family Background
Birth and Upbringing in Detroit, Michigan
The Role of Detroit's Vibrant Environment

Chapter Two: Academic Journey
High School Years and Early Academic Excellence
Stanford Graduate School of Business: Preparing for the Corporate World

Chapter Three: Career Beginnings
Initial Roles Before Microsoft
Joining Microsoft in 1980 as Its First Business Manager
Leadership in Product Strategy

Chapter Four: Journey to Leadership at Microsoft
Key Roles Before Becoming CEO

Chapter Five: Transforming Microsoft as CEO

Chapter Six: The Legacy of Steve Ballmer's Leadership
The Legacy of Leadership Transition

Chapter Seven: The Power of Philanthropy: Steve Ballmer's Post-Microsoft Impact
The Ballmer Family Foundation and Investments in Education

Chapter Eight: Legacy and Long-Term Impact: Steve Ballmer's Vision for the Future
Steve Ballmer's Legacy: A Vision for the Future

Chapter Nine: Personal Life and Values

Chapter Ten: Leadership Philosophy and Management Style
Bold Decision-Making and Risk-Taking
Emotional Intelligence and Leadership

Chapter Eleven: Challenges and Controversies
Navigating Microsoft's Transition to the Cloud

Chapter Twelve: Media Portrayal and Public Perception
Public Perception of Ballmer's Leadership
The Controversial Steve Ballmer Interviews

Chapter Thirteen: Legacy and Long-Term Impact

Chapter Fourteen: Inspirational Lessons from Steve Ballmer's Life
The Importance of Adaptability and Change
The Value of Persistence and Resilience

Chapter Fifteen: Exploring the Future: What Lies Ahead for Steve Ballmer
The Future of Technology: Potential Involvement in Tech Ventures
Leadership in a Changing World: Advocating for Better Business Practices

Conclusion

Introduction

Steve Ballmer's life is a testament to the power of energy, resilience, and vision in achieving success across multiple fields. This biography serves to provide a comprehensive understanding of his journey, capturing not only his professional achievements but also his personal growth and philosophy. By exploring the pivotal moments in his career, from joining Microsoft in its infancy to owning the LA Clippers and driving philanthropic initiatives, this book delves into how Ballmer's unrelenting passion has shaped industries and inspired countless individuals.

This work aims to celebrate Ballmer's remarkable contributions while offering a nuanced perspective on the challenges he faced and the lessons he learned along the way. Readers will gain insight into his strategic leadership during transformational periods in technology and business, as well as his impact on sports and society. Beyond his public persona as an enthusiastic leader, the book also highlights Ballmer's quieter roles as a father, husband, and advocate for transparency and economic mobility.

Steve Ballmer's career is defined by his ability to embrace change and drive innovation. As the first business manager at Microsoft, he helped build the company into one of the most powerful entities in the technology sector. During his tenure as CEO from 2000 to 2014, Microsoft's revenue tripled, and its global influence expanded. Ballmer spearheaded major projects like the Xbox gaming console and cloud computing initiatives, demonstrating his forward-thinking approach. In addition to his contributions to the tech world, Ballmer has made a significant impact in the sports arena.

His acquisition of the Los Angeles Clippers in 2014 marked a new chapter in his leadership journey. Under his ownership, the Clippers have evolved into a competitive NBA team, with innovations like the Intuit Dome enhancing the fan experience. Ballmer's influence extends beyond business and sports. As a philanthropist, he has dedicated his wealth to addressing societal challenges. Through the Ballmer Group, he supports economic mobility programs that aim to bridge systemic inequalities. His founding of USAFacts underscores his commitment to government transparency and informed civic engagement. At the core of Steve Ballmer's story are three overarching themes: leadership, innovation, and philanthropy.

His leadership journey is one of constant adaptation, whether steering Microsoft through the rise of formidable competitors like Google and Apple or navigating the complexities of sports management. Ballmer's leadership philosophy emphasizes passion, resilience, and a willingness to learn from failures—a mindset that has fueled his success in diverse fields. Innovation has been another hallmark of Ballmer's career. From transforming software into a global business to venturing into hardware and cloud computing, his forward-looking approach has left an indelible mark on the tech industry.

Even in sports management, Ballmer has leveraged his technological acumen to revolutionize team operations and fan engagement. Philanthropy represents the third pillar of Ballmer's legacy. His initiatives focus on creating opportunities for underserved communities, fostering transparency in governance, and addressing systemic challenges. Through his charitable efforts, Ballmer exemplifies how wealth can be harnessed for the greater good, inspiring others to contribute meaningfully to society. This biography seeks to weave these themes together, presenting a holistic view of Steve Ballmer's life.

It aims to offer inspiration to readers, whether they are entrepreneurs, sports enthusiasts, or individuals seeking to make a difference in their communities. The subsequent chapters of this book will provide a detailed exploration of Ballmer's life, beginning with his early years in Detroit and his academic journey at prestigious institutions like Harvard University and Stanford Graduate School of Business. Readers will witness how his formative experiences and early career shaped his leadership style and prepared him for his transformative role at Microsoft.

Ballmer's tenure at Microsoft will be examined in depth, highlighting his contributions to the company's growth and his response to industry challenges. The narrative will also cover his transition to sports management and his achievements as the owner of the LA Clippers, showcasing how he brought his business acumen to the world of professional sports. Furthermore, the book will delve into Ballmer's philanthropic endeavors, shedding light on his vision for societal impact. Through detailed accounts of his charitable projects and his establishment of USAFacts, readers will understand how Ballmer uses data-driven approaches to tackle pressing social issues.

This biography will reflect on Ballmer's enduring legacy and offer lessons from his life that can inspire future generations. From his energetic public persona to his behind-the-scenes contributions, Steve Ballmer's journey is a compelling example of how passion and determination can lead to extraordinary achievements.

Chapter One: Early Life and Family Background

Birth and Upbringing in Detroit, Michigan

Steven Anthony Ballmer was born on March 24, 1956, in Detroit, Michigan, a city renowned for its industrial might and deep connection to the American automobile industry. Detroit's bustling economy during the mid-20th century, characterized by the dominance of automotive giants like Ford, General Motors, and Chrysler, served as a dynamic backdrop to Ballmer's early life.

Growing up in a city known for its resilience and innovation undoubtedly shaped his mindset and influenced his future endeavors. Detroit's cultural diversity also played a role in shaping Ballmer's worldview. The city's working-class ethos instilled in him the values of hard work, determination, and perseverance. This environment provided Ballmer with an understanding of the importance of grit and adaptability—traits that would become essential in his career. Steve Ballmer's family background is a blend of unique cultural influences and inspiring stories.

His father, Frederic Henry Ballmer, was a Swiss immigrant who worked as a manager at Ford Motor Company. Frederic's career in one of Detroit's flagship industries brought stability to the Ballmer household and introduced young Steve to the world of business and management. Watching his father navigate corporate America provided an early glimpse into the potential for success in the business world. On his mother's side, Ballmer's heritage was rooted in Belarusian Jewish ancestry.

Beatrice Dworkin Ballmer, his mother, instilled in him a deep respect for education and intellectual pursuits. She fostered a home environment that emphasized the importance of learning, encouraging Steve to excel academically. The combination of his father's discipline and his mother's emphasis on education created a foundation for Steve's character. His parents' contrasting cultural backgrounds also gave him a broader perspective on life, helping him appreciate diversity and the value of different viewpoints. Steve Ballmer exhibited a unique combination of curiosity and competitiveness from a young age. He displayed a knack for problem-solving and critical thinking, often excelling in subjects like mathematics and science.

These early academic successes laid the groundwork for his future accomplishments in the technology sector. Growing up, Ballmer was known for his energetic personality, a trait that would later become one of his most recognizable characteristics as a leader. This energy often translated into an eagerness to take on challenges, whether in school or on the sports field. He was an avid participant in activities that allowed him to demonstrate leadership and teamwork. Despite his natural intelligence and determination, Ballmer's childhood was not without its challenges.

Like many children of immigrant families, he felt the pressure to succeed and make the most of the opportunities his parents had worked so hard to provide. This pressure drove him to aim high in all areas of his life, from academics to extracurricular activities. During his formative years, Ballmer developed an early interest in the burgeoning world of technology. While the digital revolution was still in its infancy during the 1960s, Ballmer was captivated by the potential of science and innovation to transform society. This curiosity would eventually lead him to pursue a career in technology and business. Steve Ballmer's leadership style began taking shape during his childhood.

He was often described as a natural leader among his peers, known for his ability to rally others around a shared goal. Whether organizing a neighborhood game or leading a school project, Ballmer demonstrated an innate ability to inspire confidence and motivate those around him. These early experiences laid the foundation for his later success in managing teams at Microsoft and leading the Los Angeles Clippers. Ballmer's childhood provided him with a safe space to experiment with leadership, make mistakes, and learn from them—an invaluable experience that would guide him throughout his career.

The Role of Detroit's Vibrant Environment

The city of Detroit played a pivotal role in shaping Ballmer's outlook on life. Known as the "Motor City," Detroit in the 1950s and 1960s was a hub of industrial innovation and economic activity. Growing up in such an environment exposed Ballmer to the power of innovation and the importance of building a strong work ethic. Detroit's struggles with economic downturns and social challenges also left an impression on Ballmer. Witnessing the city's resilience and determination to rebuild itself inspired him to adopt a similar mindset.

Throughout his career, Ballmer would draw on these lessons, particularly during difficult times at Microsoft and later as the owner of the LA Clippers. Steve Ballmer's family played an instrumental role in his development. His parents' emphasis on discipline and education instilled in him a deep respect for hard work and intellectual growth. Frederic Ballmer's career at Ford served as a constant reminder of the rewards of perseverance and dedication. Meanwhile, Beatrice Ballmer's encouragement of curiosity and learning helped foster her son's love for academics.

Ballmer's close relationship with his family also taught him the importance of community and connection. These values would later inform his philanthropic endeavors, particularly his focus on economic mobility and community development. Looking back at Steve Ballmer's early life, it is clear that his upbringing provided the foundation for his future success. From the influence of his parents to the lessons learned in Detroit's vibrant yet challenging environment, every aspect of his childhood contributed to shaping the leader he would become. Ballmer's early years were marked by a balance of intellectual curiosity, competitive spirit, and a deep sense of responsibility to his family and community.

These traits would remain with him throughout his life, guiding his decisions and shaping his legacy as a visionary leader in technology, sports, and philanthropy.

Chapter Two: Academic Journey

High School Years and Early Academic Excellence

Steve Ballmer's academic journey began in earnest during his high school years at Detroit Country Day School, a prestigious preparatory school known for its rigorous curriculum and focus on developing leadership skills. Ballmer's natural aptitude for mathematics and science quickly became evident, setting him apart as one of the school's top students.

His competitive nature drove him to excel not only in academics but also in extracurricular activities, where he demonstrated early signs of leadership. At Detroit Country Day, Ballmer's approach to problem-solving was marked by creativity and persistence. Teachers and peers alike recognized his ability to think critically and tackle complex challenges. These qualities earned him numerous accolades, including awards in mathematics competitions and other academic events.

Despite his academic prowess, Ballmer was not solely focused on studies. He participated actively in student organizations, honing his public speaking and interpersonal skills. These experiences helped him build confidence and prepared him for the challenges of higher education. In 1973, Steve Ballmer enrolled at Harvard University, one of the most prestigious institutions in the world. His admission to Harvard was a testament to his academic excellence and potential.

At Harvard, Ballmer chose to major in mathematics and economics, fields that aligned with his analytical mindset and interest in problem-solving. Ballmer's time at Harvard was marked by a relentless pursuit of knowledge. He thrived in the intellectually stimulating environment, taking on challenging coursework that pushed the boundaries of his understanding. His dual focus on mathematics and economics allowed him to develop a deep understanding of quantitative analysis and economic principles, skills that would later prove invaluable in his career at Microsoft. Ballmer's professors often described him as a dedicated and enthusiastic student.

His ability to grasp complex concepts quickly and apply them in practical scenarios was a defining trait. This academic rigor laid the foundation for his strategic thinking and decision-making abilities. One of the most significant aspects of Ballmer's time at Harvard was his friendship with Bill Gates, who would later co-found Microsoft. The two met in 1973 and quickly bonded over their shared love for technology and innovation. Gates, who was already working on developing software, introduced Ballmer to the world of computing, sparking a lifelong interest.

Their friendship went beyond academics. Gates and Ballmer often engaged in spirited debates about technology, business, and the future of computing. These discussions were instrumental in shaping Ballmer's understanding of the tech industry and his eventual decision to join Microsoft. When Gates decided to leave Harvard to focus on building Microsoft, Ballmer supported his decision, even though he chose to complete his studies. This early relationship with Gates would prove pivotal in Ballmer's career trajectory, leading to his eventual role as Microsoft's CEO. Beyond his academic pursuits, Ballmer was an active participant in Harvard's vibrant intellectual community.

He joined various student organizations, including the Harvard Crimson newspaper and the university's debate club. These activities helped him refine his communication skills and develop a broader perspective on global issues. Ballmer's time at Harvard also exposed him to a diverse group of peers, many of whom would go on to become influential leaders in their respective fields. This network of connections provided him with valuable insights and opportunities throughout his career.

Stanford Graduate School of Business: Preparing for the Corporate World

After graduating magna cum laude from Harvard in 1977, Ballmer briefly worked at Procter & Gamble before deciding to pursue an MBA at Stanford Graduate School of Business. His decision to attend Stanford was driven by a desire to deepen his understanding of business strategy and management. At Stanford, Ballmer focused on courses related to organizational behavior, finance, and marketing. He approached his studies with the same enthusiasm and dedication that had characterized his time at Harvard. His professors noted his ability to connect theoretical concepts with real-world applications, a skill that would later define his leadership at Microsoft.

Stanford's emphasis on innovation and entrepreneurship resonated deeply with Ballmer. The school's proximity to Silicon Valley, the epicenter of technological innovation, further fueled his interest in the tech industry. In 1980, after completing one year of his MBA program, Ballmer made the life-changing decision to leave Stanford and join Microsoft as its first business manager. This decision marked a turning point in his life, as he chose to take a risk on a fledgling software company over completing his formal education.

Ballmer's decision to join Microsoft was influenced by his friendship with Bill Gates and his belief in the company's vision. He saw the potential for Microsoft to revolutionize the tech industry and was eager to contribute to its growth. Steve Ballmer's academic journey played a crucial role in shaping his leadership style and approach to business. His time at Detroit Country Day School, Harvard University, and Stanford Graduate School of Business equipped him with the knowledge, skills, and networks necessary for success. From his rigorous study of mathematics and economics to his exposure to innovative ideas at Stanford, Ballmer's academic experiences provided the foundation for his future achievements.

These formative years were characterized by a commitment to excellence, a willingness to take risks, and an unwavering belief in the power of education to drive change. Steve Ballmer's academic journey was more than a series of educational milestones; it was a period of profound growth and self-discovery. The lessons he learned during these years, both inside and outside the classroom, shaped his character and prepared him for the challenges of leading one of the world's most influential companies.

Chapter Three: Career Beginnings

Initial Roles Before Microsoft

Before Steve Ballmer became the household name associated with Microsoft, he built a foundation of professional experiences that contributed to his leadership style and approach to business. These early roles, although not directly related to technology, played a significant part in shaping the values, skills, and work ethic that Ballmer would later bring to his work at Microsoft.

After graduating from Harvard with a degree in economics and mathematics, Ballmer joined Procter & Gamble (P&G), one of the world's largest consumer goods companies. This was his first major job after leaving academia, and it exposed him to the fast-paced world of corporate America. At P&G, Ballmer worked in the company's management training program. His role was primarily in sales and marketing, where he was tasked with managing various product lines and overseeing marketing strategies.

Although this role was far removed from the tech industry, it provided him with valuable insights into how large, complex businesses operate. He learned the importance of efficiency, managing people, and creating a competitive edge through innovation. Ballmer's time at P&G was marked by his ability to learn quickly and his drive to take on new challenges. He proved himself as a capable manager and was promoted quickly, which was a testament to his leadership potential.

However, after a few years, he felt the pull to pursue something more aligned with his long-term interests—technology. Ballmer's time at Procter & Gamble taught him a number of important lessons that would become integral to his future success at Microsoft. In particular, he learned the value of structured problem-solving, the importance of teamwork, and the need to manage both short-term objectives and long-term goals. His experience in the sales and marketing department provided him with a deep understanding of customer needs and how to effectively position products in a competitive market. Moreover, his exposure to corporate culture at P&G solidified his belief in the power of strong leadership.

Ballmer learned that in any organization, success is often determined by the quality of the people and their ability to collaborate toward a common goal. He took this lesson to heart and would later build a similar culture at Microsoft. However, after a few years at P&G, Ballmer realized that he was not truly passionate about the consumer goods industry. His aspirations were in technology, and that drive ultimately led him to seek a new opportunity.

Joining Microsoft in 1980 as Its First Business Manager

In 1980, Steve Ballmer's career took a decisive turn when he received a phone call from Bill Gates, his Harvard friend, offering him a role at Microsoft. Ballmer was hesitant at first—he was comfortable at P&G and was unsure about leaving a stable career for a company that was still relatively unknown. However, Bill Gates' passion for technology and his vision for Microsoft convinced Ballmer that this was the right move. In July 1980, Ballmer officially joined Microsoft as its first business manager. When Ballmer joined Microsoft, the company was still in its early stages. Founded in 1975 by Bill Gates and Paul Allen, Microsoft was primarily focused on creating software for personal computers, which was still a nascent industry.

At the time of Ballmer's hiring, Microsoft had fewer than 50 employees, and its products were mostly limited to programming languages and early versions of the company's famous operating systems. As business manager, Ballmer took on a wide range of responsibilities. He was tasked with managing the company's sales, marketing, and business development efforts. This was a significant role, as Microsoft was in the process of expanding its product offerings and needed someone with strong business acumen to help drive that growth.

One of Ballmer's first challenges was to help Microsoft build relationships with hardware companies that would use its software. At the time, Microsoft's software was compatible with a variety of personal computers, but the company had to convince hardware manufacturers to standardize on Microsoft's operating systems. This involved negotiating licensing agreements and building trust with potential partners, which Ballmer did with determination and energy. While Ballmer was tasked with overseeing day-to-day operations at Microsoft, he also played a key role in shaping the company's long-term vision. From the beginning, Ballmer recognized the importance of positioning Microsoft as a leader in the software industry.

He understood that to achieve long-term success, Microsoft needed to create software that was not only innovative but also user-friendly and accessible to a wide range of consumers. Ballmer's deep understanding of business strategy was instrumental in helping Microsoft navigate the competitive landscape of the tech industry. He was quick to recognize emerging trends in personal computing and software development, which helped guide the company's product development strategy.

Though the company was still small in comparison to the industry giants of the time, Ballmer's foresight and energy helped position Microsoft for future growth. His efforts to expand the company's software offerings, negotiate partnerships with hardware manufacturers, and establish a strong brand identity laid the groundwork for what would become one of the most successful technology companies in history. Ballmer's role at Microsoft quickly evolved as the company grew. His responsibilities expanded beyond business management, and he began to take on more leadership roles. As the company's sales and marketing efforts began to pay off, Ballmer played an increasingly central role in shaping Microsoft's future direction.

Leadership in Product Strategy

Ballmer's passion for technology and innovation led him to take a more active role in product strategy. Although he did not have a formal technical background, his ability to understand market needs and customer demands allowed him to contribute to Microsoft's product development efforts. He worked closely with Bill Gates and the engineering team to develop new software products, including the early versions of Windows, which would go on to become one of the most widely used operating systems in the world.

Ballmer's vision for Microsoft's growth was closely tied to his belief that personal computing would become a ubiquitous part of daily life. He recognized the transformative potential of software and its ability to shape how people interacted with technology. This vision became the driving force behind much of Microsoft's product strategy throughout the 1980s and 1990s. In addition to his work in product strategy, Ballmer also played a key role in shaping Microsoft's corporate culture. As the company grew, he emphasized the importance of building a strong, performance-driven culture.

Ballmer's management style was characterized by his high-energy approach and his ability to motivate teams to achieve ambitious goals. He fostered a competitive and results-oriented environment at Microsoft, where employees were encouraged to take risks and push the boundaries of innovation. This culture of innovation and ambition would become a hallmark of Microsoft's success in the tech industry.

Steve Ballmer's early career at Procter & Gamble and his subsequent role at Microsoft provided him with a solid foundation of skills, leadership lessons, and business acumen. His experiences in sales, marketing, and business management prepared him to take on the challenges of growing a technology company. By the time Ballmer joined Microsoft, he had already demonstrated a strong work ethic, strategic thinking, and the ability to motivate teams—qualities that would serve him well in his later role as CEO.

Chapter Four: Journey to Leadership at Microsoft

Key Roles Before Becoming CEO

Before Steve Ballmer took the helm as CEO of Microsoft in 2000, he had already played a significant role in shaping the company's growth and trajectory. His journey to leadership at Microsoft was not a straightforward one, but rather a series of important positions that helped him develop the skills and insights needed to take over one of the most successful companies in the world.

These roles were integral not only to his personal growth but also to Microsoft's success. In the early years at Microsoft, Ballmer made his mark through his work in sales and marketing. As the company sought to expand its presence in the emerging personal computer market, Ballmer helped establish Microsoft's marketing and sales strategies. These efforts were crucial in driving Microsoft's success and making its products ubiquitous across the globe. One of Ballmer's key contributions in this area was the creation of Microsoft's sales force.

In a rapidly evolving industry, Ballmer recognized that having a dedicated, talented sales team was essential to building relationships with partners and customers. He spearheaded the expansion of the sales team, helping Microsoft build a global network of partners and customers who relied on Microsoft products. Additionally, Ballmer played a pivotal role in marketing the company's flagship product—Windows. During his tenure in the marketing department, Microsoft launched several versions of Windows that would go on to define the personal computing landscape.

Ballmer's understanding of how to position and market a product in a competitive landscape was critical to Microsoft's rise to prominence. His work in marketing and sales was not just about promoting products; it was about creating a comprehensive strategy that aligned Microsoft's offerings with market needs and customer demands. In addition to his marketing contributions, Ballmer was also deeply involved in leading major product launches. One of the most notable of these was the launch of Windows 95, an event that marked a major milestone in the company's history. Windows 95 was a revolutionary product that significantly changed the way personal computers operated.

It was designed to be user-friendly, offering a graphical interface that made it easier for users to interact with their computers. Ballmer was at the center of the launch, playing a key role in managing the team and coordinating efforts across different departments. The launch was a success, and Windows 95 became one of the most widely adopted operating systems in history. It solidified Microsoft's position as the leader in the personal computer software market.

Windows 95's success was a testament to Ballmer's ability to lead large-scale projects and bring them to fruition. It also marked the beginning of a series of product launches that would continue throughout his career at Microsoft. Each of these launches required careful planning, coordination, and execution, skills that Ballmer honed during these years and would later leverage as CEO. Steve Ballmer's journey to becoming the CEO of Microsoft was marked by his steady rise through the ranks of the company. By the time he became CEO in 2000, he had already demonstrated his leadership abilities and deep understanding of the company's operations. However, his appointment was also influenced by the changing dynamics within Microsoft and the tech industry as a whole.

Transition to Leadership in the New Millennium

The appointment of Ballmer as CEO marked a new era for Microsoft. Bill Gates, the company's co-founder, had led Microsoft from its inception and had become a global icon as a result of his achievements. However, as the technology industry was evolving rapidly, Gates realized that the company needed a new leader who could take Microsoft into the next phase of its growth. In 2000, Gates decided to transition to a more hands-off role, becoming Chief Software Architect, and handed over the CEO position to Ballmer.

This transition was significant not just for Microsoft but also for the tech industry as a whole. It symbolized the shift from the first generation of technology entrepreneurs, like Gates, to a new generation of leaders like Ballmer, who were prepared to navigate the complexities of the digital age. For Ballmer, becoming CEO of Microsoft was both an exciting opportunity and a daunting challenge. He was taking over a company that was already a leader in the software industry, but with increasing competition from companies like Google, Apple, and emerging tech startups, the pressure was on to maintain Microsoft's dominance in the market.

Upon taking the CEO position, Ballmer wasted no time in setting forth his vision for Microsoft's future. He recognized that the company could not afford to remain complacent in a rapidly changing technology landscape. While Microsoft had already made its mark with products like Windows and Office, Ballmer understood that the company needed to diversify its offerings and focus on emerging technologies like cloud computing, mobile, and gaming.

Under Ballmer's leadership, Microsoft began to make strategic investments in these areas. One of the key moves was the acquisition of several companies, including the purchase of the online advertising company aQuantive in 2007. Ballmer also pushed for the development of new products like Windows Vista and Windows 7, both of which aimed to improve the user experience and maintain Microsoft's leadership in the operating system market. Additionally, Ballmer was instrumental in pushing Microsoft to focus on enterprise solutions, which helped the company expand its customer base beyond individual users and into the business sector. He was a firm believer in the idea that Microsoft's software products could help businesses streamline their operations and improve productivity.

This vision helped to solidify Microsoft's position as a global powerhouse in the tech industry. While Ballmer faced challenges in navigating the rapidly changing tech landscape, his leadership and vision were pivotal in ensuring Microsoft's continued relevance in the market. He made bold moves to ensure the company remained a leader in the personal computing space and set the stage for Microsoft's expansion into new sectors.

Steve Ballmer's journey to leadership at Microsoft was defined by his relentless work ethic, vision for the company's future, and ability to adapt to new challenges. His key roles before becoming CEO provided him with the experience and insights needed to guide Microsoft through a period of rapid change and expansion. From marketing and sales innovations to leading major product launches, Ballmer's contributions were essential to Microsoft's growth during its early years. When he became CEO in 2000, he inherited a company that was at the forefront of the tech industry, but he also faced the challenge of maintaining that dominance amid increasing competition. His strategic initiatives and vision would ultimately define his tenure as CEO, as he worked to expand Microsoft's product offerings and ensure its continued success in an increasingly complex tech world.

Chapter Five: Transforming Microsoft as CEO

Steve Ballmer's tenure as the CEO of Microsoft marked a transformative period in the company's history. Under his leadership, Microsoft continued to dominate the software industry, but Ballmer also sought to diversify its business, modernize its approach, and adapt to the rapidly changing technology landscape.

His ability to drive innovation while navigating external pressures solidified his place as one of the most influential tech leaders of the early 21st century. When Steve Ballmer became CEO of Microsoft in 2000, the company was already an established giant in the tech world, thanks largely to the success of its operating systems (Windows) and productivity software (Microsoft Office). However, under Ballmer's leadership, Microsoft experienced explosive growth that would redefine the company's financial trajectory.

Over the course of his 14-year tenure as CEO, Ballmer helped Microsoft triple its sales and double its profits. This period of expansion was driven by a combination of strategic acquisitions, new product developments, and an increased focus on cloud services. One of Ballmer's key strategies was diversifying Microsoft's product offerings. Recognizing the rapidly growing influence of the internet and new computing paradigms, he worked to extend Microsoft's reach into new markets.

For example, the company saw explosive growth in its server and tools business, which provided software solutions for enterprise clients. This market was expanding rapidly as more businesses moved toward digital and cloud-based solutions, and Ballmer understood the importance of positioning Microsoft as a leader in this space. Ballmer also focused heavily on Microsoft's international expansion. Under his leadership, the company's footprint grew globally as it capitalized on emerging markets in Asia, Latin America, and Eastern Europe. Microsoft's efforts to build a stronger presence in these regions, including expanding its software and hardware offerings, contributed significantly to the company's overall revenue growth.

Another critical aspect of Microsoft's financial success under Ballmer was the increasing dominance of the company's online services and advertising business. Ballmer saw the potential in online advertising as a revenue stream and led efforts to build a competitive digital advertising business to rival Google. Despite some early setbacks in this area, including the acquisition of the online advertising company aQuantive in 2007, which ultimately did not pay off as expected, Ballmer's vision for Microsoft's position in the online advertising market was clear.

Even though the business never matched Google's dominance, it laid the groundwork for Microsoft's continued push into internet services. While Microsoft's growth was undeniable, Ballmer faced a variety of challenges during his time as CEO. The most significant challenge was the intense competition from rivals such as Apple, Google, and later, Facebook. As the tech landscape rapidly evolved, Microsoft had to find ways to respond to the rise of new players in the market. One of the major challenges Ballmer faced was Apple's resurgence with the launch of the iPod, iPhone, and iPad.

Apple's ability to integrate hardware and software into seamless, user-friendly products made it a formidable competitor, especially in the personal computing space. Microsoft, which had traditionally relied on software and licensing, struggled to compete with Apple's growing hardware offerings, particularly in the mobile and consumer electronics markets. While Microsoft had a commanding presence in the personal computing space, Ballmer was confronted with the question of how to compete with Apple's growing mobile and tablet businesses.

The company's initial attempts to launch its own mobile operating system, Windows Phone, were met with limited success, largely due to its inability to attract developers and create a compelling ecosystem of apps. Ballmer's decision to embrace the mobile revolution through acquisitions like Nokia in 2014 was a sign of his recognition that Microsoft needed a more aggressive approach to gain ground in the mobile market. However, these efforts ultimately did not yield the desired results. At the same time, Ballmer faced growing competition from Google, whose Android operating system quickly gained traction in the mobile market.

Google's success with Android, combined with the company's dominance in search and advertising, created a formidable competitive threat to Microsoft's dominance in software. In response, Microsoft made several key acquisitions, such as the purchase of Skype in 2011 and the development of its own search engine, Bing, to attempt to counterbalance Google's influence. Additionally, Ballmer faced challenges from Facebook, which was revolutionizing the way people interacted online and rapidly gaining market share in the social media space.

Facebook's success threatened Microsoft's ability to dominate the digital space, and the company's attempts to enter the social media market, such as the acquisition of LinkedIn in 2016, were largely driven by the desire to compete with Facebook's expanding influence. Despite these challenges, Ballmer remained steadfast in his belief that Microsoft's ability to adapt and evolve would enable the company to continue to thrive. His leadership through these difficult years was a testament to his resilience and long-term vision.

Although Microsoft struggled to match the success of some of its competitors, particularly in mobile, Ballmer's focus on cloud computing, enterprise software, and hardware innovations would ensure that the company remained at the forefront of the technology industry. As the tech industry became increasingly dominated by Google, Apple, and Facebook, Ballmer's leadership style evolved to adapt to these new competitors.

Rather than attempting to directly replicate the success of these companies, he opted to continue building Microsoft's unique strengths and diversifying its product lines. While Google, Apple, and Facebook were all focused on consumer-facing products, Ballmer remained focused on the enterprise side of the business, which he believed was critical for Microsoft's long-term growth. One of Ballmer's most significant achievements during this period was the development of Microsoft's cloud computing business. Under his leadership, Microsoft made substantial investments in cloud infrastructure, culminating in the launch of Microsoft Azure in 2010.

Azure became a central part of Microsoft's overall business strategy, enabling the company to offer enterprise customers a suite of services and solutions for managing their data, applications, and digital infrastructure. The cloud business ultimately became one of Microsoft's most profitable and fastest-growing segments, and it laid the foundation for the company's future success after Ballmer's departure. Ballmer also understood the importance of consumer-facing technologies, and he led Microsoft's push into the gaming industry with the Xbox and the Surface tablet line.

The Xbox brand became a huge success, helping to position Microsoft as a leader in the gaming space and rivaling Sony's PlayStation. The launch of the Surface tablet in 2012 was also a key moment in Ballmer's leadership, signaling Microsoft's desire to enter the tablet market and compete directly with Apple's iPad. While the Surface initially struggled to gain traction, it eventually found its niche as a business-focused device, and it was an important part of Microsoft's hardware strategy. Throughout this period of fierce competition, Ballmer remained a passionate and energetic leader who focused on empowering his team and maintaining Microsoft's competitive edge.

His ability to remain optimistic in the face of challenges and his determination to invest in the company's future helped ensure that Microsoft would continue to thrive, even as new players emerged in the tech world. In addition to overseeing Microsoft's expansion and responding to external competition, Ballmer also placed a significant emphasis on fostering a corporate culture of growth and resilience. One of his core beliefs was that the company's success depended on its people, and he worked tirelessly to build a team that was capable of navigating the challenges ahead.

Ballmer's leadership style was often described as energetic, passionate, and hands-on. He was known for his ability to inspire employees, and he placed great importance on creating a culture where employees felt motivated to contribute their best work. He encouraged a fast-paced, results-oriented environment where innovation was celebrated, and failure was seen as an opportunity for growth. His leadership was central to Microsoft's ability to remain a dominant force in the tech world, even as the industry became increasingly competitive and complex. Ballmer's commitment to innovation also extended to the way he managed the company's internal teams.

He emphasized collaboration and cross-functional teamwork, recognizing that the best ideas often came from diverse perspectives. Under his leadership, Microsoft became known for its rigorous approach to product development, with teams working tirelessly to refine and improve the company's offerings.

Steve Ballmer's transformation of Microsoft was marked by both challenges and triumphs. Under his leadership, Microsoft tripled its sales and expanded into new markets, including cloud computing and gaming. Despite intense competition from companies like Google, Apple, and Facebook, Ballmer's commitment to innovation and diversification ensured that Microsoft remained a powerful force in the tech industry. His leadership during these formative years set the stage for the company's continued success, even beyond his tenure as CEO.

Chapter Six: The Legacy of Steve Ballmer's Leadership

Steve Ballmer's departure from Microsoft in 2014 marked the end of an era for the company. He had overseen its remarkable growth for more than a decade, and his leadership had guided the company through some of the most significant transformations in its history. However, as with any long tenure, Ballmer's legacy is a complex and multifaceted one. While his time as CEO was marked by bold decisions, ambitious goals, and formidable challenges, the true impact of his leadership can only be measured over time.

One of Ballmer's most lasting contributions was his vision of transforming Microsoft from a traditional software company into a broader technology services provider. Under his leadership, Microsoft transitioned from being predominantly a seller of packaged software to a company that provided cloud services, software as a service (SaaS), and other enterprise-level solutions. This shift in vision was crucial for the company's ability to stay relevant as the industry evolved and became more reliant on online services and cloud computing.

Ballmer's push toward cloud services was an essential part of this transformation. Microsoft Azure, which launched in 2010, became the centerpiece of the company's cloud computing strategy. Although the platform took time to gain traction, it eventually became one of the most successful and important parts of Microsoft's business. By the time Ballmer stepped down, Azure had established itself as a major player in the cloud industry, alongside Amazon Web Services (AWS) and Google Cloud.

Furthermore, Ballmer oversaw the introduction of Office 365, a cloud-based version of Microsoft Office, which transformed the way businesses and individuals accessed and used productivity tools. Office 365's success marked a key milestone in Microsoft's transformation into a services-based company, moving away from the traditional model of software licensing that had defined the company for decades. By shifting to a subscription-based model, Microsoft was able to secure a consistent revenue stream while providing customers with continuous updates and new features. While Microsoft's software products remained crucial to its business, the company's expanding focus on services during Ballmer's tenure would become a defining feature of its future success.

Ballmer's ability to foresee the changing landscape of the tech industry and adapt Microsoft's strategy accordingly helped ensure that the company remained competitive even as its traditional software model became less relevant in the modern world. Ballmer's tenure was also marked by a heavy emphasis on innovation and product development. As the tech industry became more dynamic and competitive, Microsoft had to constantly evolve and adapt. This meant expanding beyond its core products, such as Windows and Office, and exploring new areas of innovation.

Some of the most notable innovations during Ballmer's leadership include the Xbox gaming console, the Surface tablet, and the introduction of Windows 8. The Xbox, which had been launched in 2001, became a huge success during Ballmer's leadership, with the company eventually establishing itself as a key player in the gaming industry. The Xbox brand became synonymous with high-quality gaming experiences and drove Microsoft's success in the entertainment and media sectors. Ballmer's vision for Xbox was more than just about gaming; he saw it as an entry point into the broader entertainment ecosystem, integrating television, movies, and streaming services into the platform.

This broader vision for Xbox would eventually influence the development of Microsoft's entertainment strategy, particularly through its later efforts to push for integration with cloud services and digital content. Another significant product that Ballmer helped to launch was the Surface tablet, which debuted in 2012. The Surface was Microsoft's attempt to compete directly with Apple's iPad in the tablet market. Although the initial iteration of the Surface struggled to gain widespread adoption, it marked a pivotal moment in Microsoft's shift towards hardware development.

The Surface lineup would continue to evolve under Ballmer's successor, Satya Nadella, but it was during Ballmer's tenure that the idea of Microsoft as a hardware company began to take root. This move into hardware signaled a change in the company's strategy, reflecting its desire to control not just the software but the entire computing experience for its customers. Windows 8, which was released in 2012, was another ambitious attempt by Ballmer and his team to revolutionize the personal computing experience. Windows 8 was designed to bring a more mobile-friendly interface to desktop PCs, with an emphasis on touch functionality.

While Windows 8 was met with mixed reviews, it was an example of Ballmer's willingness to push the boundaries of Microsoft's traditional operating system. It also represented an effort to modernize the company's offerings in response to the increasing dominance of mobile devices and tablets. Although not all of the products Ballmer introduced during his time as CEO were immediate successes, his willingness to take risks and invest in new technologies helped position Microsoft as a forward-thinking company that was willing to innovate.

Even when products like Windows 8 or the original Surface struggled, they laid the groundwork for future successes in areas such as cloud computing, hardware, and mobile services. While Ballmer's leadership was widely seen as successful in many respects, it was not without its controversies. His leadership style was often characterized by his energetic and aggressive approach, which occasionally led to criticism. Ballmer was known for being a highly emotional and sometimes combative leader, traits that both inspired loyalty and generated criticism. He was known for his intense focus on driving Microsoft's performance and would often push his team to achieve ambitious goals.

While his enthusiasm and drive were admired by many, they also led to a culture at Microsoft that could be seen as overly competitive and, at times, intolerant of failure. One of the most notable criticisms of Ballmer was his handling of the company's mobile strategy. Despite the growing importance of mobile computing, Microsoft struggled to gain a foothold in the mobile phone market under Ballmer's leadership. The company's attempts to enter the mobile space, including the launch of Windows Phone, were met with limited success.

Ballmer's decision to acquire Nokia's handset business in 2014 was an attempt to address this weakness, but it ultimately did not yield the desired results. Microsoft's inability to compete with Apple and Google in the mobile market is often cited as one of the key shortcomings of Ballmer's tenure. Another controversial decision during Ballmer's leadership was the acquisition of aQuantive, an online advertising company, in 2007. The acquisition, which was valued at $6 billion, was intended to help Microsoft compete with Google in the digital advertising space. However, the acquisition did not deliver the expected results, and Microsoft eventually wrote off the majority of the investment.

This misstep led to questions about Ballmer's judgment in making large, high-risk acquisitions. Despite these controversies, Ballmer's ability to manage Microsoft through periods of uncertainty and transition cannot be understated. He was unafraid to make bold moves and take risks, even when faced with significant opposition. His tenure was marked by a constant balancing act between the pressures of maintaining Microsoft's dominant position in the software market while also adapting to the rapidly changing tech landscape.

The Legacy of Leadership Transition

One of the most important aspects of Ballmer's legacy was his decision to step down as CEO and hand the reins of Microsoft to Satya Nadella in 2014. Ballmer's decision to retire was seen by many as a natural progression, as the company was at a crossroads. Nadella, who had been with Microsoft for over two decades, was seen as a strong candidate to lead the company into the next phase of its growth. Ballmer's decision to step aside and allow a new leader to take Microsoft into the future speaks to his self-awareness and his desire to ensure that the company continued to thrive even after his departure.

Nadella's leadership would go on to usher in a new era for Microsoft, focusing on cloud computing and artificial intelligence. However, the foundations of these efforts were laid during Ballmer's time as CEO. Nadella has often credited Ballmer's leadership for positioning the company for success in the cloud era, as Ballmer's investments in Azure and cloud infrastructure helped set the stage for Microsoft's current dominance in the cloud space. In the years following his retirement, Ballmer has remained active in philanthropy and investing.

He is widely respected for his contributions to the tech industry and his leadership of Microsoft during a period of immense change. His legacy continues to influence Microsoft's direction, even as the company evolves under new leadership. Steve Ballmer's legacy as CEO of Microsoft is defined by his remarkable drive for growth, innovation, and resilience. His leadership helped transform the company from a software giant into a diversified technology company, with a strong presence in cloud computing, gaming, and enterprise services. While his tenure was marked by significant challenges and controversies, his ability to navigate the rapidly changing tech landscape ensured that Microsoft remained a dominant force in the industry.

Ballmer's legacy lives on in the company's continued success and the transformation of the tech industry as a whole.

Chapter Seven: The Power of Philanthropy: Steve Ballmer's Post-Microsoft Impact

After stepping down as the CEO of Microsoft in 2014, Steve Ballmer turned his attention to new ventures, including philanthropy, and continued to influence both the business world and his community. While his time at Microsoft was defined by his role as a tech leader, his post-Microsoft years have cemented his legacy as a philanthropist, investor, and advocate for social causes.

One of the key vehicles through which Steve Ballmer channels his philanthropic efforts is the Ballmer Group, which he co-founded with his wife, Connie Ballmer. The Ballmer Group is dedicated to supporting nonprofits that focus on issues such as economic mobility, education, and creating opportunities for underprivileged communities, particularly in the United States. Their overarching goal is to drive systemic change and improve the life outcomes for individuals and families facing poverty.

The Ballmer Group works closely with organizations that have a measurable impact on communities, with a focus on breaking the cycle of poverty through initiatives such as workforce development, youth mentorship, and educational reform. Steve and Connie have both personally committed significant funds to various initiatives through the Ballmer Group, emphasizing their belief in creating pathways to success for all people, especially those who face systemic barriers.

Ballmer's focus on economic mobility reflects a personal value he holds dear: the idea that anyone, regardless of their background, should have access to opportunities for success. This commitment is particularly evident in the Ballmer Group's focus on creating support structures for youth, which aims to empower young people to overcome adversity and realize their full potential. In particular, much of the work done through the Ballmer Group supports underrepresented groups, such as low-income and minority populations, working to break down the barriers that prevent them from achieving their goals.

The Ballmer Family Foundation and Investments in Education

Another major facet of Ballmer's philanthropic endeavors is his work with the Ballmer Family Foundation. This foundation focuses primarily on improving educational opportunities for young people in the U.S. The Ballmer Family Foundation has made substantial investments in several educational organizations, with a specific focus on providing access to quality education for children from low-income households. In addition to offering grants, the foundation also partners with local school districts to help improve teaching quality and student outcomes.

One of the foundation's most notable partnerships is with The Seattle Foundation, where Ballmer made significant contributions to programs aimed at improving educational access and success. The foundation's work includes initiatives that directly support the development of high-performing charter schools in underserved areas, providing children with access to a high-quality education regardless of their socioeconomic status. Through its efforts, the Ballmer Family Foundation has become one of the most impactful contributors to educational reform in the Pacific Northwest.

In addition to education, Ballmer's philanthropic interests extend to advocacy for youth development programs. He is a vocal supporter of the need for comprehensive after-school and mentorship programs that empower young people to achieve success. Through the Ballmer Group and the Ballmer Family Foundation, he has advocated for and supported projects that provide mentorship, leadership development, and career skills to youth across the country.

These investments reflect Ballmer's belief that one of the most powerful ways to combat poverty and inequality is through equitable access to education and opportunities for personal development. Steve Ballmer's acquisition of the Los Angeles Clippers in 2014, shortly after stepping down from his role at Microsoft, marked the beginning of a new chapter in his public life. Ballmer purchased the Clippers for $2 billion, making him one of the highest-profile sports owners in the world. Under his leadership, the Clippers have undergone a transformation, not just on the court, but also in terms of their relationship with the Los Angeles community. From the outset of his ownership, Ballmer made it clear that he would approach his new role with the same energy, enthusiasm, and drive for excellence that defined his tenure at Microsoft.

He immediately set about improving the team's performance and building a new, modern arena for the Clippers that would rival other sports venues in the country. However, Ballmer's vision for the Clippers extended beyond basketball. He sought to create a deeper connection with the Los Angeles community, especially in underserved neighborhoods where access to sports, education, and career opportunities is limited.

In addition to his work on improving the team's facilities, Ballmer has made substantial investments in local programs designed to support young people. Through his ownership of the Clippers, Ballmer has funded youth sports initiatives and community engagement projects, offering local children and families access to sports facilities, mentorship, and career development opportunities. The Clippers' ownership has provided Ballmer with a unique platform to contribute to the broader community, blending his love for sports with his commitment to improving the lives of young people in Los Angeles. Ballmer has also used his ownership position to advocate for improving access to affordable housing and economic development in Los Angeles.

As part of his vision for the Clippers, he is dedicated to investing in the region's future growth and prosperity, particularly in areas where economic development has been slow or stagnant. His willingness to invest in the community, both financially and through initiatives designed to improve the lives of Angelenos, has helped position Ballmer as not just a sports owner but also a community leader in the city.

D. Investing in Data and Civic Tech for Social Impact

Beyond education, sports, and community development, Steve Ballmer has become increasingly focused on using data and technology to advance social causes. In 2017, he launched the Ballmer Group's Investment in Data and Technology, an initiative that aimed to apply data analytics and technology to improve government efficiency and services for underserved populations. Ballmer has been vocal about the potential for data-driven solutions to address social inequality and help governments and organizations make more informed decisions.

One of the areas where Ballmer has focused his efforts is the development of data-driven solutions to improve public services, such as child welfare, healthcare, and social services. Through partnerships with tech companies, nonprofits, and government agencies, Ballmer is helping to implement data systems that provide insights into where resources should be allocated to have the most impact. This initiative reflects Ballmer's belief in the transformative power of technology to address complex societal challenges, and his dedication to bringing technological solutions to sectors that traditionally lag behind in digital transformation.

In his work with civic tech, Ballmer has also advocated for the use of technology to strengthen democracy and increase government transparency. He has invested in platforms that promote public participation and allow citizens to have a more active role in the decision-making process. His advocacy for improving government effectiveness through data and tech has been widely praised, positioning him as a leader in the emerging field of civic technology. Ballmer's philanthropic efforts and investments have had a profound impact on many sectors, particularly in the areas of education, social mobility, and community development.

His approach to giving—one that is rooted in partnership, collaboration, and leveraging the power of technology—has influenced countless organizations and individuals. Ballmer's ability to mobilize resources and drive systemic change in a range of fields sets him apart from other tech billionaires who also pursue philanthropic endeavors. His emphasis on measuring success and ensuring that his philanthropic initiatives are data-driven and results-oriented has influenced how other philanthropists view their own efforts.

Ballmer's work with the Ballmer Group and the Ballmer Family Foundation has set a high standard for those in the tech world who seek to use their wealth to make a difference. It's a standard that prioritizes long-term impact, sustainability, and the empowerment of underserved communities. Furthermore, Ballmer's commitment to transparency in his philanthropic work has encouraged others to be more open about their charitable activities. His recognition of the importance of accountability in philanthropy has led to a more thoughtful approach to giving, ensuring that funds are used efficiently and effectively. Ballmer's impact is an example of how wealth, when coupled with a strong sense of purpose, can create lasting change.

A soft life has been defined by a commitment to using his resources and influence to create lasting social change. Through the Ballmer Group, the Ballmer Family Foundation, his ownership of the Clippers, and his investment in technology for civic good, Ballmer has cemented his reputation as one of the most impactful philanthropists of his generation. His ability to drive change in both the private and public sectors reflects a personal mission to empower underserved communities, improve social mobility, and invest in solutions that will shape a more just and equitable future.

Chapter Eight: Legacy and Long-Term Impact: Steve Ballmer's Vision for the Future

As Steve Ballmer continues to reshape the landscape of technology, sports, and philanthropy, his legacy remains a subject of considerable discussion.

Throughout his career, his work has not only made a profound impact on the industries he has touched but has also shaped the way we think about the intersection of business, social responsibility, and innovation. Steve Ballmer's leadership journey is often contrasted with that of his predecessor, Bill Gates, yet the two have had complementary roles in making Microsoft the global giant it is today. Ballmer's vision and strategic decision-making helped guide Microsoft into an era of rapid expansion and, at times, tumultuous change.

One of the most notable elements of Ballmer's leadership at Microsoft was his unwavering commitment to growth and market dominance, which led to successful acquisitions, such as the purchase of Skype and Nokia's mobile business, though some of these investments have been scrutinized in hindsight. Nevertheless, Ballmer's legacy at Microsoft can also be viewed through the lens of transformation.

He was instrumental in shifting Microsoft from a primarily software-focused company to one that embraced cloud computing, mobile technology, and enterprise solutions. These shifts in strategy ensured Microsoft's continued relevance as the tech landscape evolved. Ballmer understood that for a company to remain at the forefront of innovation, it must constantly adapt to change—a lesson he has taken with him into his post-Microsoft life. The philosophical shift in Ballmer's leadership style after his tenure at Microsoft is equally significant. His work in philanthropy and community engagement, particularly in his support of education and workforce development, reflects a more human-centered approach to leadership.

No longer solely driven by the pressures of managing a multi-billion-dollar tech empire, Ballmer has been able to focus on how he can make a positive difference in people's lives. His shift from corporate titan to socially conscious philanthropist underscores the importance of evolving leadership and recognizing broader societal challenges. As he reflects on his own career, Ballmer has often expressed a belief in servant leadership—the idea that leaders should empower those around them and focus on the needs of others.

This philosophy has guided his philanthropic endeavors, where he applies the same principles that made him a successful businessman to improving communities and building systems of support for the marginalized. He often emphasizes that leadership isn't just about profit margins and market share, but about making a positive difference in people's lives. Steve Ballmer's contributions to technology are immeasurable, but his vision for the future extends beyond just technological innovation. In his post-Microsoft years, he has become a passionate advocate for using technology to address social challenges.

As the founder of the Ballmer Group, Ballmer has made it his mission to harness the power of data and digital tools to improve public services, increase government transparency, and break down barriers to opportunity for disadvantaged communities. One of the areas where Ballmer sees the greatest potential for technology to create lasting change is in education. He has often expressed concern about the inequality of educational opportunities in the United States, particularly among underprivileged children.

Ballmer has invested in a wide range of education-related initiatives, such as charter schools, mentorship programs, and after-school initiatives, all of which leverage technology to enhance the learning experience. Ballmer's vision is to ensure that every child, regardless of their socioeconomic status, has access to the tools and opportunities necessary for success. Through his philanthropic organizations, such as the Ballmer Family Foundation, Ballmer is pushing for the digitization of educational resources to create an accessible and equitable learning environment for all students. He is particularly focused on closing the digital divide, which disproportionately affects low-income and minority students.

By making educational materials more widely available and incorporating technology into the classroom, Ballmer believes that we can help bridge the gap between the haves and the have-nots in education. Beyond education, Ballmer also believes that digital technology can be used to address a variety of societal issues, from healthcare access to public safety to environmental sustainability.

Ballmer's emphasis on technology as a means of solving complex, real-world problems sets him apart as a visionary who sees beyond the commercial potential of tech to its broader social implications. He views social good as an integral component of technology's evolution, and he is committed to driving that change through his investments, advocacy, and partnerships with other leaders in the tech community. Steve Ballmer's ownership of the Los Angeles Clippers has been a pivotal chapter in his post-Microsoft career, but it is more than just a financial investment in a professional sports team. Under Ballmer's leadership, the Clippers have flourished not only in terms of their on-court performance but also in their engagement with the Los Angeles community.

Ballmer has made it clear that he views the Clippers as a vehicle for creating positive change in the city, particularly for young people in underserved communities. Through his ownership of the Clippers, Ballmer has focused on creating an inclusive culture that extends beyond basketball. His commitment to using sports as a platform for youth empowerment and community engagement has been evident in the organization's partnerships with local charities and schools.

Ballmer's philanthropic work with the Clippers includes supporting youth sports leagues, providing scholarships for underserved students, and improving access to recreational facilities. He sees the Clippers as an opportunity to help shape future generations, both through their engagement with the team and their participation in community-building activities. Ballmer also views his ownership as a chance to redefine the relationship between professional sports teams and the cities they represent. In an era where many teams and owners are criticized for prioritizing profit over community impact, Ballmer has emphasized the importance of investing in the community and building strong, lasting connections with fans.

He is determined to leave a legacy of positive social change through his work with the Clippers, and his efforts are starting to pay off in meaningful ways. Under his leadership, the team has become a symbol of empowerment, with the emphasis on diversity, inclusion, and support for local causes. While Steve Ballmer's contributions to the tech world are already well-documented, his continuing work in the field of philanthropy will likely prove to be just as influential.

As one of the world's most notable tech entrepreneurs, Ballmer has paved the way for others to leverage technology for social good, and his work continues to inspire others to follow suit. Ballmer's success with the Ballmer Group and other philanthropic ventures demonstrates that giving back does not have to be separate from business success. He has shown that it is possible to combine social impact with entrepreneurial spirit, and that the skills and resources gained in business can be directly applied to the pursuit of positive change. As the world becomes increasingly focused on issues like social justice, sustainability, and equity, Ballmer's model of purpose-driven philanthropy will continue to influence future generations of philanthropists, business leaders, and activists.

As the digital landscape evolves, Ballmer's emphasis on data-driven philanthropy and his advocacy for technology's role in public policy will likely influence future discussions on how to tackle global challenges. He is not only setting an example in how to use one's wealth and influence for good but also in how corporate leaders can balance business with social responsibility in a meaningful way.

Steve Ballmer's Legacy: A Vision for the Future

Steve Ballmer's legacy is still being written, but his vision for the future is clear: he wants to continue driving positive social change, using his vast wealth and influence to make the world a better place. Whether it's through his leadership at Microsoft, his investments in education and technology, or his role as the owner of the Los Angeles Clippers, Ballmer has demonstrated a commitment to leaving a lasting, positive impact on the world. As the world grapples with issues such as inequality, climate change, and technological disruption, Ballmer's work reminds us of the importance of using our resources and talents to address the challenges that affect our communities.

His belief in the power of technology, education, and community engagement continues to guide his efforts as he works to shape a more equitable and sustainable future. His legacy will be one of innovation, empowerment, and purpose-driven leadership, setting a powerful example for generations to come.

Chapter Nine: Personal Life and Values

Steve Ballmer's journey in the business world is not only characterized by his extraordinary accomplishments but also by the values and personal experiences that shaped his life outside of work. While many may know him for his leadership at Microsoft and his passion for the LA Clippers, understanding his personal life offers important insights into the kind of individual he is, beyond the corporate persona.

His relationships, interests, and life choices have all played an essential role in his development as a leader and philanthropist. At the core of Steve Ballmer's personal life is his strong connection to family. Family plays a central role in shaping his worldview, and his relationship with his wife, Connie Snyder, exemplifies the values that guide him. Steve and Connie have been together for decades, having married in 1990. Their relationship has been marked by mutual respect, shared ambitions, and a partnership that balances personal growth with professional pursuits.

Connie Snyder, who is known for her work in public relations and her role in various philanthropic endeavors, has been a steady source of support throughout Ballmer's career. Their marriage has not only been a partnership in the personal sense but also in the philanthropic domain. Both Steve and Connie have a deep commitment to giving back to society, with many of their charitable efforts aligned.

Connie's influence is visible in the philanthropic initiatives that the Ballmer Group, the couple's charitable foundation, has undertaken to improve economic mobility, especially for underserved communities. In addition to his marriage, Ballmer's relationship with his children, Sam and Annie, is another key aspect of his personal life. His role as a father has been an important one, and despite his demanding career, Ballmer has always prioritized time with his family. He has spoken about how his children have influenced his perspective on life, providing him with the grounding and perspective needed to balance the high demands of his professional life. Though private, Steve Ballmer's family life offers a rare glimpse into the man behind the corporate executive.

His commitment to his wife and children underscores the importance of family as a source of inspiration and emotional support, helping him navigate the highs and lows of his career. Beyond his professional and family commitments, Steve Ballmer is known for his wide range of personal interests, some of which may come as a surprise to many. His passion for sports, particularly basketball, is well-known, and his ownership of the LA Clippers speaks to the depth of this interest.

For Ballmer, sports are not just a business venture; they represent an opportunity to foster community, inspire passion, and create a lasting legacy. His exuberance for basketball is mirrored by his active involvement in the Clippers' management, where he has sought to improve the team's performance, fan engagement, and overall standing in the NBA. Outside of basketball, Ballmer has a deep appreciation for a variety of other sports, including tennis and football. His affinity for competition, teamwork, and performance extends beyond his work at Microsoft and into his personal life. Ballmer has often spoken about the lessons he has learned from sports, particularly in terms of resilience, teamwork, and the importance of staying grounded despite setbacks.

His active lifestyle is not only a reflection of his competitive spirit but also a key element of his approach to maintaining his well-being in an often-demanding world. Another area of personal interest for Ballmer is music. Although not as publicly known for his musical talents, Ballmer has often shared his love for music in interviews, speaking about how it serves as an important outlet for relaxation and creativity. Whether it is listening to music or engaging in activities like attending concerts, Ballmer's appreciation for art forms beyond the boardroom adds to his complexity as a person.

Moreover, Ballmer's love for travel has also been a significant part of his life. His travels, both for business and pleasure, have allowed him to experience different cultures and gain new perspectives. This broad exposure has informed his thinking about global markets, technology, and leadership. He has often mentioned how travel has helped him keep a broad and inclusive worldview, which is critical in the globalized economy where Microsoft and his other ventures operate. In many ways, Steve Ballmer's ability to balance his personal life with his high-stakes professional career speaks to his understanding of what truly matters in life.

Throughout his career, he has maintained a steadfast belief that success is not just about accumulating wealth or power but about living a well-rounded life. While his business accomplishments are legendary, Ballmer has never been one to prioritize work over his health, family, or passions. In interviews, he has frequently emphasized the importance of finding harmony between the demands of the business world and the need for self-care, time with loved ones, and pursuing hobbies.

One of the key aspects of Ballmer's philosophy when it comes to balance is his ability to delegate and trust his team. As a leader, Ballmer understood the importance of surrounding himself with talented individuals who could take on key responsibilities. This approach allowed him to focus on the bigger picture while also ensuring that his personal life did not fall by the wayside. In a world where work-life balance is often a struggle for high-powered executives, Ballmer's ability to manage both has been an inspiration to many aspiring leaders. Additionally, his transition from Microsoft CEO to the owner of the LA Clippers marked a significant shift in his personal life and how he approached work-life balance.

As he moved from the tech world to sports ownership, Ballmer found new ways to channel his energy into an area he is passionate about, yet one that offers a different pace and set of challenges. This shift allowed him to continue contributing at a high level but with a renewed focus on something he truly loves. Steve Ballmer's personal life is more than just an afterthought to his business career; it has been integral to his success and the person he is today.

His relationships with his family, his commitment to maintaining a healthy work-life balance, and his diverse range of interests all contribute to a well-rounded individual who has made a lasting impact on the world. The values and principles that Steve Ballmer holds dear are reflected in how he interacts with his loved ones, approaches personal hobbies, and balances his ambitions with the reality of everyday life. These elements of his personal life provide crucial insights into his leadership style and the success he has achieved over the years. They are a testament to the fact that, for Steve Ballmer, success is not only measured by professional achievements but by the relationships he builds and the passions he pursues outside of the business world.

Chapter Ten: Leadership Philosophy and Management Style

Steve Ballmer's leadership philosophy and management style have been shaped by a unique combination of his experiences, personal values, and his dynamic approach to business. Throughout his tenure at Microsoft and beyond, Ballmer has demonstrated a management style characterized by high energy, decisiveness, and a strong focus on people and culture.

His approach to leadership, although sometimes seen as unconventional, has proven highly effective in achieving extraordinary business results. One of the most defining characteristics of Steve Ballmer's leadership style is his boundless energy and enthusiasm. His famous "Ballmer Energy" was a hallmark of his time at Microsoft, often seen in his charismatic speeches, keynote addresses, and day-to-day interactions with employees. Ballmer is known for his exuberant personality, which has frequently been described as infectious.

His energy was not just about maintaining an exciting atmosphere, but also about inspiring others to feel the same passion and dedication to the company's mission. Ballmer believed that a leader's energy could significantly influence a team's performance. By demonstrating his own commitment and passion for the company's success, he aimed to motivate his employees to give their best, creating a culture where energy and enthusiasm were seen as vital ingredients for success.

This energy was not only directed outward but also harnessed inward, helping Ballmer sustain his focus and drive even during times of intense pressure or corporate challenges. While many leaders in Silicon Valley tend to adopt a more subdued, cerebral approach to management, Ballmer was a leader who led by emotion and raw energy. He saw passion as a key differentiator in the competitive tech industry, believing that a motivated and energetic team could accomplish anything. Ballmer's approach was certainly distinctive, but it proved to be highly effective in energizing Microsoft's workforce during periods of transition and growth.

Ballmer's leadership philosophy placed a strong emphasis on people and organizational culture. He firmly believed that the success of a company is rooted in the talent and dedication of its employees. Under his leadership, Microsoft's focus shifted from a purely technology-driven approach to a more people-oriented philosophy, where the skills, development, and satisfaction of employees were at the forefront of strategic decision-making.

Ballmer made it clear that leadership wasn't just about managing the company's financial success but also about nurturing an environment where employees feel valued and empowered. He understood that people are the most important asset of any organization and that their engagement and satisfaction directly impacted the overall performance of the business. This people-centric approach involved making significant investments in employee development, fostering a culture of collaboration, and ensuring that leaders within the company were approachable and supportive of their teams. One of the cornerstones of his leadership was the idea of meritocracy. Ballmer believed in promoting individuals based on their capabilities, work ethic, and performance, rather than seniority or political maneuvering.

He emphasized the importance of giving people the opportunity to grow and take on leadership roles, provided they demonstrated the necessary skills and drive to succeed. His commitment to a meritocratic culture helped foster an environment where top talent was continuously nurtured and empowered to achieve greatness.

Bold Decision-Making and Risk-Taking

Steve Ballmer's leadership style was characterized by a strong willingness to make bold decisions, even when they involved significant risks. Ballmer was known for his decisiveness and his ability to take action in situations where others might have hesitated. This was particularly evident during his time as CEO of Microsoft when he made a series of high-stakes decisions that would shape the company's future. One of the most notable examples of Ballmer's bold decision-making was his decision to push Microsoft into new markets, such as the mobile industry, despite the company's late entry. While many critics believed Microsoft had missed the boat with mobile, Ballmer's vision for the company's future led him to invest heavily in the development of Windows Mobile and later the acquisition of Nokia's handset business.

Although these efforts didn't always yield the desired results, they exemplified Ballmer's willingness to take calculated risks in pursuit of long-term growth. Ballmer's approach to decision-making also involved being highly proactive and not shying away from making tough calls. For instance, when it became clear that Microsoft's Internet Explorer was falling behind rivals such as Google Chrome and Mozilla Firefox, Ballmer was quick to refocus the company's efforts on improving its browser technology, ultimately leading to the development of Microsoft Edge.

He didn't wait for competition to outpace Microsoft; instead, he pushed the company to innovate and catch up in a rapidly changing environment. Despite the occasional setbacks, Ballmer's risk-taking and bold decision-making earned him a reputation as a leader who wasn't afraid to challenge the status quo. His approach to leadership was driven by a belief in taking action, even when the outcome was uncertain, and that bold moves were necessary for staying competitive in a fast-paced industry. While Ballmer was known for his energetic, bold style, he also understood the importance of collaboration and teamwork in achieving corporate success.

He placed a great emphasis on empowering his leadership team and encouraging cross-departmental collaboration. Ballmer recognized that in order to innovate and grow, Microsoft needed to break down silos within the organization and foster an environment where teams could work together toward common goals. One of the ways Ballmer promoted collaboration was through a series of initiatives aimed at improving communication and teamwork among departments.

He encouraged open dialogue between product teams, marketing, and engineering, making it clear that no one group could succeed in isolation. This collaborative approach not only helped improve the company's internal dynamics but also contributed to the development of innovative products that were well integrated across various functions. Ballmer also placed great importance on transparency within the organization. He regularly communicated the company's goals, challenges, and strategic initiatives to all employees, ensuring that everyone understood their role in Microsoft's overall mission. This transparency helped build trust among employees and made them feel more connected to the company's success.

Emotional Intelligence and Leadership

Although known for his high energy and aggressive leadership style, Ballmer also demonstrated a high degree of emotional intelligence. Emotional intelligence, which refers to the ability to understand and manage one's emotions as well as recognize and influence the emotions of others, played a key role in Ballmer's success as a leader. Ballmer's emotional intelligence allowed him to read the room during crucial moments, whether in meetings with his leadership team or during major company announcements.

He had the ability to gauge the mood and energy of the team, adjusting his approach accordingly. If a situation called for motivation, he would be the first to jump in with enthusiasm. If a more reflective or strategic approach was needed, he could adapt his style to fit the circumstances. One of the best examples of Ballmer's emotional intelligence came during times of crisis. In moments of intense pressure, such as when Microsoft faced competition from Apple and Google, Ballmer remained calm and focused, offering reassurance and direction to his team.

His ability to manage his own emotions and those of others helped keep morale high and allowed Microsoft to continue pushing forward despite external challenges. Steve Ballmer's leadership philosophy and management style were key factors in his success at Microsoft and his ongoing achievements. His combination of high energy, passion, people-centric leadership, bold decision-making, and emotional intelligence helped propel Microsoft to new heights and shaped its corporate culture for years to come.

While his leadership style may have been unconventional at times, it proved to be effective in driving innovation, empowering employees, and positioning Microsoft for long-term success. Ballmer's legacy as a leader goes beyond his business accomplishments; it encompasses the people he inspired, the organizational culture he fostered, and the lessons he imparted to those who worked with him. His leadership philosophy continues to serve as a valuable blueprint for aspiring leaders in all industries, offering timeless insights into the importance of passion, collaboration, and decisive action in the pursuit of success.

Chapter Eleven: Challenges and Controversies

Steve Ballmer's tenure as CEO of Microsoft was not without its challenges and controversies. As one of the most prominent figures in the tech industry, Ballmer was often at the center of major debates concerning Microsoft's strategy, his leadership style, and his decisions that ultimately shaped the company's future.

Navigating Microsoft's Transition to the Cloud

One of the most significant challenges that Ballmer faced during his time as CEO was the shifting landscape of the tech industry, especially the move from traditional software to cloud computing. When Ballmer took the helm in 2000, Microsoft was already a dominant force in the world of personal computing, with its Windows operating system and Office suite being widely used across the globe. However, as cloud computing began to emerge as the next big trend, Microsoft found itself facing a new and unfamiliar frontier.

While companies like Amazon and Google were quick to capitalize on cloud infrastructure, Microsoft was slow to fully embrace this new business model. Ballmer's reluctance to dive headfirst into the cloud was initially met with skepticism. He famously dismissed cloud computing as an "overhyped" trend in the early 2000s, a stance that many critics viewed as shortsighted. Microsoft continued to rely heavily on its legacy software products, such as Windows and Office, and struggled to adapt to the changing technological landscape.

By the time Ballmer recognized the importance of the cloud, competitors like Amazon Web Services (AWS) had already established themselves as leaders in the space. While Ballmer eventually shifted Microsoft's focus to cloud computing, including the launch of Azure in 2010, the company struggled to catch up. Under Ballmer's leadership, Microsoft's efforts in the cloud space were seen as reactive rather than proactive. Many analysts argued that Microsoft had missed the opportunity to be a first mover in the cloud industry, and this delay in the transition to the cloud remained a point of contention throughout Ballmer's tenure.

The decision to push forward with the cloud strategy later in Ballmer's leadership did help Microsoft regain some ground, but the controversy surrounding the company's slow response to the cloud industry continued to haunt the company throughout his final years as CEO. Critics argued that the delay cost Microsoft valuable time and resources, and the company found itself constantly playing catch-up with its competitors. Another major challenge Ballmer faced was the release of Windows Vista in 2007.

Although Windows Vista was marketed as the next big leap forward for the Windows operating system, it was plagued by a series of technical issues and shortcomings that severely impacted its success. Windows Vista was intended to offer a more visually appealing interface, better security, and enhanced features over its predecessor, Windows XP. However, the operating system received widespread criticism for its high system requirements, performance issues, compatibility problems, and security vulnerabilities. Ballmer and his leadership team were forced to defend Vista in the face of mounting negative feedback.

The operating system was heavily criticized by consumers and businesses alike, many of whom were hesitant to upgrade from the more stable and reliable Windows XP. Vista's lackluster reception was seen as a major setback for Microsoft, especially considering the amount of time and resources that had been invested in its development. The controversy surrounding Vista not only damaged the reputation of the operating system but also cast doubt on Microsoft's ability to innovate and deliver products that met the needs of its users.

While Windows Vista's failure was not entirely Ballmer's fault, it became a point of contention during his leadership. Critics questioned his management of the product's development and his handling of the negative press surrounding Vista. Although Microsoft eventually released Windows 7, which was seen as a major improvement over Vista, the damage had been done. Windows Vista's failure contributed to the growing perception that Microsoft, under Ballmer's leadership, was losing its edge in the competitive software market. Perhaps one of the most significant controversies during Ballmer's tenure was Microsoft's inability to gain a foothold in the mobile industry.

As companies like Apple and Google began to dominate the smartphone market with their iPhones and Android devices, Microsoft struggled to establish a competitive presence in the mobile space. Ballmer's decision to focus on Microsoft's mobile operating system, Windows Phone, was met with mixed reactions. Windows Phone, which debuted in 2010, was initially seen as a promising alternative to iOS and Android, with its unique tile-based interface and integration with other Microsoft products.

However, despite positive reviews from tech critics, Windows Phone failed to gain significant market share. Microsoft's attempts to differentiate itself in the mobile space were unsuccessful, as consumers and developers gravitated toward the more established ecosystems of Apple and Google. Ballmer's decision to acquire Nokia's handset business in 2014 was another controversial move. At the time, Nokia was struggling in the mobile market, and many analysts questioned the wisdom of investing in a company that had been left behind by the industry's rapid evolution. While Ballmer believed the acquisition would strengthen Microsoft's position in the mobile market, it ultimately proved to be a failed investment.

The Nokia acquisition did little to boost Windows Phone's market share, and it became clear that Microsoft was unable to compete with Apple and Google in the mobile space. The failure to successfully execute a mobile strategy under Ballmer's leadership became one of the most enduring criticisms of his time as CEO. Despite his efforts to make Microsoft a major player in mobile, the company was unable to catch up with its competitors, and its mobile initiatives were ultimately abandoned after Ballmer's departure.

The inability to secure a lasting presence in the mobile industry remains a significant mark on Ballmer's legacy. While Steve Ballmer was widely admired for his energy, passion, and decisiveness, his management style was also a source of criticism. His intense, sometimes abrasive leadership style was not always well received by employees or outside observers. Ballmer's reputation for being highly demanding and occasionally volatile led to tensions within the company, and some employees felt that he could be difficult to work with.

Ballmer's emphasis on performance and results often meant that he expected employees to work long hours and prioritize Microsoft's goals above their personal lives. While this drive for excellence led to success in many areas, it also contributed to a corporate culture that was seen as stressful and overly competitive. Some critics argued that Ballmer's focus on achieving short-term objectives sometimes came at the expense of employee well-being and long-term strategic planning.

Additionally, Ballmer's tendency to make quick, decisive moves without fully consulting with his leadership team was seen as a weakness by some. While his decisiveness was an asset in certain situations, it could also result in hasty decisions that were not fully thought through. For instance, his rapid pivot to focus on the cloud and his controversial decisions around Windows Vista and the Nokia acquisition raised questions about his decision-making process and whether he always took the necessary time to weigh the long-term consequences. Another significant challenge Ballmer faced in his later years as CEO was the issue of succession.

As Microsoft entered a new era in which technology and business models were rapidly evolving, Ballmer's leadership began to be questioned by some shareholders and analysts who felt that the company needed fresh leadership to navigate the challenges of the 21st century. After announcing in 2013 that he would step down as CEO, Ballmer faced intense scrutiny over the process of selecting his successor.

The selection of Satya Nadella as Microsoft's next CEO in 2014 was met with widespread approval, as Nadella was seen as a strong candidate who could guide Microsoft through its transformation into a cloud-first company. However, the process of finding a successor was not without its controversies, as many critics questioned whether Ballmer had done enough to prepare for a smooth leadership transition. Steve Ballmer's tenure as CEO was filled with challenges and controversies, from Microsoft's slow transition to the cloud to the failure of Windows Vista and the company's inability to break into the mobile market. Despite these setbacks, Ballmer's leadership was instrumental in guiding Microsoft through a period of tremendous growth and transformation.

While some of his decisions were controversial, they reflected his bold, decisive leadership style and his willingness to take risks.

In the face of these challenges, Ballmer remained determined to push Microsoft forward, navigating the company through turbulent waters with his characteristic energy and drive. His tenure may have been marked by setbacks, but it was also a period of significant progress, and his legacy continues to influence Microsoft's strategic direction to this day.

Chapter Twelve: Media Portrayal and Public Perception

Steve Ballmer's time as CEO of Microsoft was one of constant media scrutiny and public attention, with his leadership style and decisions frequently making headlines. As a prominent figure in the tech world, Ballmer's actions, both in and out of the boardroom, were closely analyzed and often became the subject of intense public debate.

From his energetic, often animated public persona to his controversial business decisions, Ballmer's media portrayal played a significant role in shaping his public perception. One of the most iconic aspects of Steve Ballmer's public image was his exuberant, high-energy demeanor. His boisterous personality, loud voice, and animated gestures earned him the nickname "the Ballmer effect." This persona, which he carried both in public appearances and in interviews, stood in stark contrast to the more reserved leadership styles of some of his Silicon Valley counterparts, such as Apple's Steve Jobs or Google's Eric Schmidt.

While Ballmer's energy was often seen as a symbol of his enthusiasm and commitment to Microsoft, it was also a source of ridicule for some. The media frequently highlighted his larger-than-life presence, often focusing on moments where his passion seemed to veer into the realm of the absurd. For example, his infamous "developers, developers, developers!" speech in 2000, in which he repeatedly shouted the word "developers" while pumping his fists, became a viral moment in the tech world.

While his message about the importance of developers to Microsoft's future was legitimate, the dramatic delivery of the speech led many to mock him, portraying him as a man too caught up in theatrics. Despite the ridicule, Ballmer embraced his public persona, often using humor and self-awareness to deflect criticism. His larger-than-life energy became a defining characteristic of his leadership style, and many saw it as both an asset and a liability. The media's portrayal of Ballmer was often polarized. On the one hand, his passion and enthusiasm were viewed as signs of his deep commitment to Microsoft and its success.

On the other hand, his loud and often over-the-top presentations were seen as evidence of an inability to maintain the calm, composed leadership expected of someone in his position. Critics sometimes described Ballmer as a figure who was more concerned with his own image than the company's strategic direction, and the media frequently portrayed him as an erratic and unpredictable leader.

Public Perception of Ballmer's Leadership

Throughout Ballmer's tenure as CEO, public perception of his leadership was shaped by his bold decisions, his style of management, and his public persona. While Ballmer was widely respected for his intelligence and his deep understanding of Microsoft's inner workings, his leadership decisions were often subject to fierce debate. The media and analysts often framed his time as CEO in terms of successes and failures, with a focus on the results of his leadership rather than the underlying strategy. Many critics argued that Ballmer's leadership was marked by missed opportunities. As Microsoft faced increasing competition from companies like Apple and Google, some saw Ballmer as a leader who failed to adapt quickly enough to the changing tech landscape.

The company's struggles to transition to the cloud, its inability to break into the mobile market, and the failure of Windows Vista were often cited as key points of criticism. As Ballmer's tenure progressed, public perception of his leadership became more negative, and many viewed him as a CEO who was too slow to respond to the challenges posed by new technologies and business models. However, there were also many who saw Ballmer as a leader who navigated Microsoft through difficult times.

Under his leadership, Microsoft remained a profitable company and continued to generate billions in revenue. Ballmer made several bold acquisitions, including the purchase of Skype and the creation of the Surface tablet, both of which were seen as attempts to modernize the company. Despite the criticisms, some public figures and analysts argued that Ballmer was simply operating in an environment where even the most successful companies faced immense pressure to adapt to rapidly changing markets. The public's perception of Ballmer was also influenced by his relationship with the media. While he was not as media-savvy as some of his Silicon Valley peers, he was generally open to interviews and public appearances.

Ballmer's willingness to engage with the press, despite his often controversial decisions, made him a more approachable figure than other tech executives. However, his interactions with the media were not always smooth. Ballmer's candid, sometimes blunt nature meant that he was frequently caught in the crossfire of media scrutiny, and his responses to criticism were often perceived as defensive or combative.

The Controversial Steve Ballmer Interviews

One of the most defining aspects of Ballmer's media presence was his willingness to engage in public debates and interviews, even when the questions posed to him were difficult or uncomfortable. Throughout his career, Ballmer gave numerous interviews to journalists and tech analysts, many of which were marked by his direct and occasionally combative responses. These interviews often made headlines, especially when Ballmer's answers challenged the prevailing narrative about Microsoft's future. For example, in a 2007 interview with BusinessWeek, Ballmer famously declared that "Apple's business model is doomed" and that Microsoft would continue to dominate the personal computing market.

This statement was widely criticized, as Apple's rise in the mobile and personal computing markets had already begun to disrupt Microsoft's dominance. Ballmer's confident yet dismissive comments about Apple and other competitors were seen as emblematic of his sometimes overconfident and combative nature. These remarks only fueled the media's portrayal of him as a leader who was out of touch with the changing dynamics of the tech industry. Ballmer's relationship with the media also faced challenges due to his tendency to take criticism personally.

In several instances, when media outlets criticized Microsoft's performance or questioned his leadership decisions, Ballmer responded in a manner that some saw as defensive and even hostile. For example, after the negative reception of Windows Vista, Ballmer took to the media to defend the operating system, publicly stating that "the criticism was unfair" and that the product would ultimately succeed. However, this defensive approach only contributed to the media's perception that Ballmer was unwilling to acknowledge his mistakes and adapt to criticism.

Despite the controversies surrounding his interviews, Ballmer's media presence was a testament to his willingness to stand by his decisions, even in the face of adversity. While some viewed this as a sign of his confidence and determination, others saw it as evidence of a leader who was unwilling to listen to feedback and change course when necessary. When Ballmer announced in 2013 that he would step down as CEO of Microsoft, the media response was a mix of surprise, curiosity, and skepticism.

While many had anticipated that Ballmer's tenure might end sooner rather than later, the news still sparked intense media attention. As Ballmer prepared to leave the company, the media began to assess his legacy, and public opinion about his leadership became more complex. In the years following his departure from Microsoft, Ballmer's public perception began to shift. Many of the criticisms of his leadership, particularly regarding the company's struggles in the mobile and cloud markets, were reevaluated in the context of Microsoft's broader strategy. Some analysts began to argue that Ballmer's decisions, while not always popular, had been made with the long-term health of the company in mind.

The media began to recognize that Ballmer's leadership had played a crucial role in keeping Microsoft profitable during a time of intense competition and change in the tech industry. In the years since his departure from Microsoft, Ballmer has largely remained out of the spotlight, with his media appearances becoming more infrequent. However, his involvement in the purchase of the Los Angeles Clippers basketball team in 2014 offered a glimpse into his post-Microsoft life.

Ballmer's acquisition of the Clippers was seen as a bold move, and the media praised him for his commitment to improving the team and its performance. The public's perception of Ballmer as a businessman who could succeed outside of the tech world helped shift his legacy from being one of controversy to one of resilience and adaptability. Steve Ballmer's portrayal in the media and his public perception have evolved significantly over the years. His energetic and sometimes controversial leadership style, combined with his bold decisions, often put him at the center of media scrutiny. While Ballmer's tenure at Microsoft was marked by both successes and failures, his ability to engage with the media and stand by his decisions left a lasting impression on the public.

As time has passed, many have come to appreciate the complexities of his leadership, recognizing both his flaws and his achievements. Ballmer's legacy, shaped in part by his media portrayal and public perception, continues to influence how he is remembered in the tech world.

Chapter Thirteen: Legacy and Long-Term Impact

Steve Ballmer's legacy as the CEO of Microsoft and his long-term impact on the tech industry, business leadership, and philanthropy are multifaceted. Ballmer's tenure at Microsoft was a period marked by intense growth and innovation, but also by missed opportunities and challenges.

While some of his decisions were met with harsh criticism, many of his actions and choices have proven to be more influential and valuable in retrospect, shaping the course of the company and the technology industry in profound ways. One of the most enduring aspects of Steve Ballmer's legacy is the continued success of Microsoft in the years following his departure from the company in 2014. Under Ballmer's leadership, Microsoft transitioned from a dominant player in personal computing software to a more diversified technology company, focused on cloud computing, gaming, and enterprise services.

While Ballmer's time as CEO was not without its challenges, particularly in the mobile and tablet sectors, his long-term vision for Microsoft helped position the company for success in the cloud computing era. After Ballmer's departure, Satya Nadella succeeded him as CEO and refocused Microsoft on cloud computing and artificial intelligence. Nadella's leadership has undoubtedly been transformative for the company, with Microsoft Azure emerging as one of the leading cloud platforms worldwide.

However, the foundation for this success was laid during Ballmer's time at the helm, particularly through strategic investments in cloud technologies like Azure and the acquisition of LinkedIn in 2016. Though it was Nadella who ultimately capitalized on these investments, it was Ballmer's foresight in diversifying Microsoft's portfolio that set the stage for the company's continued dominance in the tech industry. Under Ballmer, Microsoft also made several bold acquisitions that would have lasting effects. One of the most significant was the purchase of Skype in 2011 for $8.5 billion. While some critics initially questioned the acquisition, fearing that it was overpriced, the deal paid off in the long term as Skype became an integral part of Microsoft's communications ecosystem.

Ballmer's acquisition strategy, though at times criticized, played a key role in expanding Microsoft's reach and maintaining its relevance in a rapidly changing technological landscape. Moreover, Microsoft's dominance in the gaming industry can also be attributed to Ballmer's leadership. The Xbox, which debuted in 2001, became one of the most successful gaming consoles in history. Under Ballmer, the Xbox brand grew into a major player in the gaming industry, and the Xbox Live service became a key driver of online gaming and digital media consumption.

Today, Microsoft's gaming division remains one of the company's most important sources of revenue, thanks in large part to the investments and strategic decisions made during Ballmer's tenure. Despite the continued success of Microsoft in the years following his departure, Ballmer's legacy as CEO is still the subject of debate. Some view him as a visionary who steered Microsoft through some of its most challenging periods and made tough decisions that ultimately benefited the company. Others argue that his leadership was marked by missed opportunities and strategic missteps, particularly in the areas of mobile and touch computing, where Microsoft was unable to replicate the success of competitors like Apple and Google.

One of the most frequent critiques of Ballmer's leadership was his handling of the mobile phone market. While Apple's iPhone and Google's Android operating system quickly became dominant forces in the smartphone space, Microsoft struggled to gain a foothold in the market. Ballmer's insistence on focusing on the Windows Mobile platform, which failed to keep pace with the rapidly changing smartphone landscape, is often cited as one of his biggest strategic mistakes.

The company's delayed response to the mobile revolution, coupled with a failure to fully embrace the rise of touch-based computing, led to Microsoft's eventual exit from the mobile phone market. However, some analysts argue that Ballmer's decision to avoid fully committing to the mobile market was not entirely misguided. Ballmer was a CEO who made decisions based on the long-term health of the company, and he recognized that Microsoft's core business was built on software and services for personal computers, rather than hardware. His reluctance to rush into mobile was not necessarily a failure but rather a reflection of his desire to maintain Microsoft's focus on its core strengths, particularly in enterprise software and services.

Ballmer's leadership legacy is also characterized by his efforts to push Microsoft into new markets. His focus on enterprise services, such as Office 365 and Microsoft Dynamics, helped transform Microsoft into a cloud-first company, even before the term became a buzzword in the tech industry. Ballmer's investments in cloud technologies, though not always immediately profitable, were crucial in positioning Microsoft for success in the cloud computing era.

His decision to pivot Microsoft's focus from traditional software to cloud-based services was an important move that helped the company remain relevant and competitive in an increasingly digital world. Beyond his impact on Microsoft, Steve Ballmer's legacy is also evident in his approach to corporate leadership and management. Ballmer's leadership style, which was often described as intense, hands-on, and demanding, has influenced many corporate leaders who followed him. Ballmer was known for his enthusiasm and passion, as well as his deep understanding of Microsoft's operations. His hands-on management style, coupled with his willingness to take risks and make bold decisions, helped shape the culture of Microsoft during his time as CEO.

Ballmer's leadership philosophy was based on the belief that companies should embrace change and take calculated risks in order to stay ahead of competitors. He was known for his unrelenting focus on growth and his belief that Microsoft's success was ultimately dependent on the ability to innovate and adapt to new challenges. Under his leadership, Microsoft was constantly pushing for new product launches, strategic acquisitions, and the development of new technologies.

However, Ballmer's management style was not without its drawbacks. His aggressive approach to competition, combined with his sometimes brash personality, led to tensions within the company. His interactions with employees and stakeholders were often described as high-pressure, and his demand for excellence sometimes created a culture of fear. Critics argue that this style of leadership may have contributed to some of the internal struggles and organizational challenges Microsoft faced during Ballmer's tenure. Despite the criticisms, many of Ballmer's management practices have become more widely accepted in the corporate world. His focus on growth, innovation, and the pursuit of new markets has influenced the way many companies approach leadership today.

Ballmer's ability to maintain Microsoft's profitability during times of intense competition and technological disruption is a testament to his leadership skills and vision. In addition to his work at Microsoft, Steve Ballmer's legacy is also defined by his philanthropic efforts. In 2014, Ballmer and his wife, Connie, established the Ballmer Group, a foundation dedicated to supporting organizations that work to improve the lives of low-income families.

The foundation's focus is on advancing economic mobility, supporting educational initiatives, and helping to reduce poverty in communities across the United States. Ballmer's commitment to philanthropy reflects his belief that individuals and organizations have a responsibility to give back to society. His decision to use his wealth to fund initiatives that promote social good has become an integral part of his post-Microsoft legacy. The Ballmer Group is focused on supporting programs that provide opportunities for underserved communities, particularly in the areas of education, workforce development, and family economic stability. Ballmer's philanthropic efforts are not just limited to the United States.

In 2014, he also joined the Giving Pledge, a campaign initiated by Warren Buffett and Bill Gates that encourages wealthy individuals to donate the majority of their wealth to charitable causes. Through his philanthropic endeavors, Ballmer has positioned himself as a philanthropist who is committed to making a difference in the world, using his resources to tackle some of the most pressing social issues of our time.

Steve Ballmer's legacy is one that is marked by both successes and challenges. While his leadership of Microsoft was not without its controversies, his impact on the company and the tech industry as a whole is undeniable. From his efforts to transition Microsoft into a cloud-first company to his hands-on management style, Ballmer's influence on the tech world continues to be felt long after his departure. His philanthropy and commitment to social causes further contribute to a legacy that is characterized by a passion for growth, innovation, and giving back to society. Steve Ballmer's lasting impact on the world of business, technology, and philanthropy ensures that his legacy will be remembered for years to come.

Chapter Fourteen: Inspirational Lessons from Steve Ballmer's Life

Steve Ballmer's life and career offer numerous lessons, not only for business leaders but also for anyone striving to overcome challenges and make a meaningful impact in their field. His journey from a Harvard graduate to the CEO of one of the world's largest tech companies, followed by his ventures into philanthropy and sports ownership, serves as an inspirational story of perseverance, growth, and transformation.

One of the most striking aspects of Steve Ballmer's leadership was his unrelenting passion and enthusiasm for Microsoft and its products. Known for his energetic speeches and lively presentations, Ballmer's infectious energy played a critical role in rallying employees and stakeholders behind his vision for the company. His famous on-stage moments, such as shouting "developers, developers, developers!" in an effort to emphasize the importance of building a strong developer community, became symbolic of his relentless drive to push Microsoft forward.

Ballmer's passion was not confined to his public persona; it was embedded in his management style and his approach to decision-making. He believed that passion for one's work was essential to achieving great success. Whether it was championing new technologies, driving innovation, or securing new acquisitions, Ballmer's enthusiasm was a constant motivator for those around him. His energy not only inspired Microsoft's workforce but also set a tone for the company's culture during his tenure.

For aspiring leaders, the lesson here is clear: passion and enthusiasm are critical ingredients for success. When leaders are genuinely excited about their work, it becomes contagious, motivating others to follow suit. Ballmer's ability to convey his enthusiasm for Microsoft's products and vision played a key role in the company's success, particularly during periods of uncertainty and competition. Passion breeds commitment and perseverance, both of which are essential for overcoming challenges and achieving long-term goals.

The Importance of Adaptability and Change

Steve Ballmer's career was marked by constant change and adaptation. Throughout his time at Microsoft, he witnessed the tech industry undergo rapid transformations, with the rise of the internet, the advent of mobile computing, and the explosion of cloud technologies. As the world of technology evolved, so too did Microsoft's approach to its products and services.

Ballmer's decision to focus on cloud computing, despite the company's historic reliance on software for personal computers, is a testament to his ability to adapt to changing circumstances. While some of his early decisions were met with skepticism, his embrace of cloud technologies in the early 2000s ultimately paid off. Ballmer's foresight in recognizing the potential of the cloud, combined with his willingness to invest heavily in the technology, positioned Microsoft for success in the coming decades. The lesson here is that adaptability is essential for success in any industry. The world is constantly changing, and leaders who fail to evolve with the times risk being left behind.

Ballmer's ability to embrace change, make bold decisions, and guide Microsoft through periods of technological disruption serves as a reminder that success is often determined by one's ability to pivot and adjust to new realities. Steve Ballmer was not afraid to make bold decisions, even when they came with considerable risks. Throughout his time at Microsoft, he made several high-profile acquisitions, including the purchase of Skype for $8.5 billion in 2011.

At the time, many critics questioned whether the acquisition was a wise move, as Skype had yet to prove its long-term viability. However, Ballmer saw the potential for Skype to become a key part of Microsoft's strategy for communication and collaboration, and his willingness to take the risk ultimately paid off. Ballmer's decision to take risks was also evident in his approach to new product launches. While some of his product bets, such as the Windows Phone, did not achieve the success he had hoped for, his willingness to invest in emerging technologies demonstrated a forward-thinking mindset. Even in the face of failure, Ballmer maintained a focus on innovation and progress, and he used his setbacks as learning experiences to refine Microsoft's strategy going forward.

For those looking to succeed in business, one of the most important lessons from Ballmer's life is the value of taking calculated risks. In a rapidly changing world, leaders must be willing to make bold moves in order to stay competitive. However, risk-taking must be accompanied by careful analysis and a willingness to learn from failure. Ballmer's approach to risk was guided by his belief that failure was a natural part of the innovation process, and that the rewards of success often outweighed the costs of failure.

The Value of Persistence and Resilience

Steve Ballmer's journey to success was not without its setbacks. While he experienced considerable success during his tenure at Microsoft, he also faced criticism, internal conflicts, and moments of doubt. The company's struggles with mobile and its failure to capture the market in the way that Apple and Google had were significant challenges that Ballmer had to navigate. Additionally, Ballmer's aggressive management style and some of his decisions, such as his focus on Windows Mobile, led to moments of tension within Microsoft. However, what set Ballmer apart was his resilience in the face of adversity.

Rather than shying away from challenges, he confronted them head-on, using them as opportunities for growth. Even during times when Microsoft faced criticism or slowdowns in growth, Ballmer remained focused on his long-term vision for the company. His persistence allowed him to weather difficult periods and make decisions that, in hindsight, positioned Microsoft for future success. The lesson here is that resilience and persistence are vital qualities for anyone striving to achieve their goals.

Success is rarely achieved without obstacles, and the ability to bounce back from setbacks and continue pushing forward is what separates successful leaders from those who falter. Ballmer's ability to stay focused on his mission, even when faced with failure, serves as a powerful reminder that persistence is key to overcoming challenges. Steve Ballmer understood the importance of surrounding himself with talented individuals and fostering a strong team culture at Microsoft. He was known for his focus on recruiting the best talent, pushing his teams to excel, and ensuring that employees were motivated and aligned with the company's goals.

During his tenure, Ballmer made significant efforts to build a diverse and inclusive workplace, recognizing that a wide range of perspectives was crucial for driving innovation and problem-solving. Ballmer's leadership style also emphasized the importance of collaboration and teamwork. While he was known for being a hands-on and sometimes intense leader, he also placed a high value on team dynamics and collective success. He understood that no single individual could achieve success on their own and that the strength of Microsoft lay in the capabilities of its people working together.

For anyone in a leadership position, the lesson from Ballmer's approach is clear: building and leading a strong team is essential for long-term success. Leaders must prioritize talent acquisition, create a culture of collaboration, and ensure that their teams have the resources and support they need to excel. A strong, motivated team is often the key to turning visionary ideas into reality. After leaving Microsoft, Steve Ballmer's philanthropic efforts have become a major part of his legacy. Through the Ballmer Group, he has focused on addressing social challenges, particularly in the areas of economic mobility and educational opportunity for low-income families.

Ballmer's belief in the power of giving back to the community is a central theme in his post-Microsoft life. Ballmer's philanthropic work provides a valuable lesson in the importance of using one's success and resources to make a positive impact on the world. While many successful individuals focus solely on personal wealth and achievement, Ballmer has demonstrated that true fulfillment comes from helping others and creating opportunities for those in need.

His commitment to social causes underscores the idea that success should not be measured solely by financial achievement but by the positive change one can bring to the world. Steve Ballmer's life and career are a testament to the power of passion, adaptability, risk-taking, persistence, and philanthropy. From his leadership at Microsoft to his post-retirement philanthropic endeavors, Ballmer has demonstrated that success is not just about financial achievement, but about making a meaningful difference in the world. The lessons from his life are timeless, offering inspiration to anyone seeking to create a lasting impact in their chosen field.

Through his example, Ballmer reminds us that achieving greatness requires not only intelligence and strategy but also an unwavering commitment to one's vision, a willingness to take risks, and a dedication to helping others. His story serves as an inspiration for future leaders, entrepreneurs, and philanthropists, showing that with passion, resilience, and a focus on the greater good, anyone can make a lasting mark on the world.

Chapter Fifteen: Exploring the Future: What Lies Ahead for Steve Ballmer

Steve Ballmer's remarkable career has spanned decades of unprecedented change in the technology, business, and philanthropic landscapes. From his time at Microsoft, where he helped steer the company through its most pivotal years, to his post-Microsoft ventures, including his role as the owner of the Los Angeles Clippers and his focus on philanthropy, Ballmer's journey has been marked by bold decisions and strategic foresight.

However, as with any leader of his caliber, the question remains: What lies ahead for Steve Ballmer? Since acquiring the Los Angeles Clippers in 2014, Ballmer has revolutionized the way the franchise operates. His investment in the Clippers has not only transformed the team's performance on the court but also its culture, infrastructure, and relationship with the fans. Under his leadership, the Clippers have become a more competitive force in the NBA, and Ballmer's passionate commitment to the team's success has reshaped the sports ownership model.

Moving forward, it is clear that Ballmer's influence on the Clippers will continue to grow. With a focus on building a new arena for the team—something that has been a long-term vision for him—Ballmer is positioning the Clippers to be at the forefront of the NBA's next era. The new state-of-the-art arena, which is set to open in 2024, is a symbol of his commitment to the team and its fans. Ballmer has made it clear that the Clippers are not just another NBA franchise for him, but a project he is deeply invested in, both emotionally and financially.

What's next for Ballmer in sports? With the Clippers' new home set to be one of the most advanced arenas in the country, Ballmer's focus will likely turn to leveraging technology and fan engagement to enhance the overall experience for spectators. Whether through innovations in in-game entertainment, immersive experiences, or expanding the global reach of the team, Ballmer's tech-savvy approach to sports ownership will likely influence how future sports franchises operate. While Ballmer's legacy in business and sports continues to evolve, his commitment to philanthropy is a central aspect of his post-Microsoft life.

Through the Ballmer Group, Steve and his wife Connie have committed their wealth and time to addressing key social issues, particularly in the realm of economic mobility for low-income families. The Ballmer Group's focus has been on helping children from disadvantaged backgrounds, ensuring they have access to education, housing, and career opportunities. Looking ahead, it is expected that Ballmer will continue to expand his philanthropic footprint, especially in the areas of education and economic empowerment.

Given his strategic mindset, it's likely that Ballmer will explore new, innovative approaches to addressing social inequality—whether that's by investing in scalable education programs, advocating for policy changes, or collaborating with other philanthropists and organizations to achieve systemic change. Additionally, his deep connection to the city of Los Angeles, combined with his financial resources, may allow him to play a larger role in transforming the city's socio-economic landscape. The Ballmer Group's ongoing work in education and economic mobility is just the beginning of what could be a lifelong commitment to improving the lives of marginalized communities across the United States.

The Future of Technology: Potential Involvement in Tech Ventures

Ballmer's career has been intertwined with the rapid evolution of the technology industry. As a key player in Microsoft's transformation from a software giant to a leader in cloud computing and other high-growth areas, Ballmer has seen firsthand how technology can disrupt industries, change markets, and revolutionize our daily lives.

Although Ballmer stepped down from Microsoft's leadership in 2014, his involvement in the technology space is far from over. It is entirely possible that he will re-enter the tech world in some capacity—whether as an investor, advisor, or even through the creation of new ventures. Given his passion for innovation and his deep understanding of the industry, Ballmer's ability to identify the next big opportunity in tech remains a hallmark of his leadership. As the technology landscape continues to evolve with advancements in artificial intelligence, machine learning, blockchain, and other emerging fields, Ballmer's experience and insights could provide invaluable contributions to these industries.

In particular, his understanding of cloud computing, software development, and consumer-facing technologies could make him a key player in shaping the next generation of tech innovation. It wouldn't be surprising if Ballmer, in collaboration with other tech pioneers, launches or invests in a startup that addresses a major global challenge, from climate change to healthcare to cybersecurity.

Leadership in a Changing World: Advocating for Better Business Practices

Steve Ballmer's leadership philosophy has been largely shaped by his time at Microsoft, where he championed a culture of collaboration, innovation, and perseverance. However, in today's rapidly changing business environment, where technology, globalization, and societal issues intersect, the role of business leaders is evolving. There is increasing pressure on corporate leaders to address issues such as climate change, diversity and inclusion, and ethical business practices, while also delivering financial results. Looking ahead, Ballmer may become a more vocal advocate for ethical leadership and corporate responsibility.

His previous work, including his philanthropic initiatives, suggests that he is deeply concerned about using business as a force for positive social change. As such, it is possible that Ballmer will take on a larger role in advocating for responsible business practices that balance profitability with social good. Whether through thought leadership, partnerships, or public speaking, his influence could shape the way business leaders approach issues like environmental sustainability, fair wages, and ethical governance.

In a world where consumers are increasingly demanding more from the companies they support, Ballmer's expertise in building strong, values-driven organizations could prove to be an invaluable resource for companies striving to adapt to this new reality. Given his track record of making bold decisions and thinking outside the box, it's likely that Ballmer will continue to challenge traditional business norms in ways that push for a more sustainable and inclusive future. Steve Ballmer's future is one that is marked by continued influence, innovation, and social good. As a philanthropist, sports owner, and potential re-entering figure in the tech space, Ballmer is poised to continue making a lasting impact on multiple industries.

His contributions to Microsoft, the Los Angeles Clippers, and various social causes already form the foundation of his legacy, but it is clear that his story is far from over. What lies ahead for Steve Ballmer? It's not just about what he can achieve in the next decade or two, but also about how his legacy will continue to influence future generations of leaders, philanthropists, and entrepreneurs. Ballmer has proven that with passion, vision, and the courage to take risks, great things can be accomplished.

Whether through the Clippers, his philanthropic endeavors, or future ventures, it is evident that Steve Ballmer's journey is a testament to the power of leadership, innovation, and service to the greater good. As we look to the future, Steve Ballmer's influence will continue to be felt not only through his business ventures but also through the impact he has on the lives of countless individuals. His leadership in sports, technology, and philanthropy has set a benchmark for others to follow. The future is undoubtedly bright for Steve Ballmer, and whatever path he chooses to take, his legacy of transformational leadership will endure for years to come.

Conclusion

Steve Ballmer's extraordinary journey through the worlds of technology, business, sports, and philanthropy paints the picture of a man whose life has been defined by vision, commitment, and an unwavering belief in the potential for transformation. From his pivotal role in Microsoft's meteoric rise to his present-day impact as the owner of the Los Angeles Clippers and a passionate philanthropist, Ballmer's career is a remarkable story of growth, leadership, and reinvention.

Throughout this biography, we have explored the many facets of Steve Ballmer's life: his early years, his rise to the top of Microsoft, his leadership style, and the challenges he faced both professionally and personally. We have seen how his approach to management and decision-making has left a lasting mark on the companies and organizations he's led. His legacy, in both the tech and sports industries, is undeniable. Yet beyond his corporate accomplishments, it is his deeper commitment to philanthropy, his passion for uplifting communities, and his pursuit of creating lasting societal change that makes his story truly inspiring.

Steve Ballmer's legacy is undeniably tied to his role in shaping the modern tech industry. As the former CEO of Microsoft, he presided over the company during one of its most challenging and transformative periods. His tenure was marked by significant moments: the expansion of Microsoft's product offerings, the company's push into the cloud computing space, and its shift from a software-driven company to a more diverse technology conglomerate. While Ballmer's leadership was at times controversial, it was never devoid of impact.

His ability to execute strategic shifts in a rapidly changing environment was a hallmark of his leadership, and this adaptability continues to serve as a model for future business leaders. What sets Ballmer apart from many other business leaders is his capacity to bring people together around a common goal. Whether it was the employees at Microsoft, the fans of the Los Angeles Clippers, or the organizations benefiting from his philanthropic endeavors, Ballmer's influence has extended beyond the boardroom. He's shown that success is not solely about profits; it's about the positive changes a leader can create in the lives of others.

His leadership philosophy, centered on fostering collaboration, driving innovation, and supporting others' growth, will continue to serve as an invaluable blueprint for leaders in various industries. Another defining feature of Steve Ballmer's journey is his visionary thinking. When Ballmer joined Microsoft in the early 1980s, the company was already on its way to becoming a key player in the software industry. However, it was Ballmer's foresight that helped propel Microsoft to even greater heights.

He believed in the power of software to shape the world and drove Microsoft's efforts to dominate operating systems, office productivity software, and later, cloud computing. His ability to see the bigger picture, even in moments of adversity, was a critical factor in the company's long-term success. This visionary thinking did not end with his departure from Microsoft. As the owner of the Los Angeles Clippers, Ballmer has demonstrated that his business acumen is not limited to tech. His investment in the team's future, his commitment to building a new, state-of-the-art arena, and his focus on creating a fan-first experience all speak to his enduring belief that anything can be transformed with the right vision and effort.

For the business world, Ballmer's ability to identify potential, nurture it, and create lasting value is a powerful reminder that leadership is about more than just making decisions in the present moment. It's about shaping the future—whether that future is in the tech sector, sports, or philanthropy. Perhaps one of the most inspiring aspects of Steve Ballmer's story is his commitment to philanthropy and social change. After leaving Microsoft, Ballmer dedicated much of his time and wealth to causes that matter deeply to him.

Through the Ballmer Group, he has worked tirelessly to improve the lives of low-income families, particularly in the areas of education and economic mobility. His efforts to address these systemic issues have had a profound impact on communities across the United States, and his influence in this space is only expected to grow. What sets Ballmer's philanthropic work apart is his hands-on approach. He doesn't just write checks; he engages with the organizations he supports, seeking to understand the problems they face and working directly with them to find solutions. This commitment to being actively involved in social causes is an important reminder of the power that individuals—especially those with significant resources—can have in driving meaningful change.

Ballmer's philanthropic work also reflects his broader worldview: that leadership is not just about success in business, but about contributing to the greater good. His efforts in education, housing, and economic empowerment align with his desire to create opportunities for people who have historically been left behind. In doing so, he's helping to build a more just and equitable society, one that offers hope and possibility to all its citizens. As we look to the future, it's clear that Steve Ballmer's impact is far from over.

His work as the owner of the Clippers will continue to shape the world of sports ownership and fan engagement. His ongoing philanthropic endeavors will likely transform more communities, ensuring that the issues of economic mobility and education remain at the forefront of the national conversation. And with his deep understanding of the technology industry, it's entirely possible that Ballmer will continue to be a key player in shaping the next generation of tech innovation. Though Ballmer has already accomplished so much, his journey is still in its early stages. His leadership, his commitment to making a difference, and his drive to innovate will ensure that his influence will continue to be felt for decades to come.

The life and career of Steve Ballmer are defined by one central theme: transformation. Whether it was transforming Microsoft into one of the most influential companies in the world, transforming the Los Angeles Clippers into a competitive NBA team, or transforming communities through his philanthropy, Ballmer has demonstrated time and again that true leadership is about creating positive, lasting change. His story is a testament to the power of vision, the importance of adaptability, and the potential for business leaders to make a difference in the world. As Ballmer continues to chart his path forward, the world can only look on with anticipation, knowing that his best work may still be ahead of him.

Made in United States
Troutdale, OR
03/14/2025